Praise for *It's a God Thing*

"With their new book, *It's a God Thing*, I believe K-LOVE and my friend Don Jacobson will call friends of Jesus everywhere to look for His capers around the world! Do you know why God involves Himself in our lives? Because God is love and love does!"

— Bob Goff, author of the *New York Times* bestseller *Love Does*

"If there is one thing that God wants us to understand, it is total dependence on Him. Sometimes we find that we are completely wiped out and feel there is nowhere else to turn. God tells us to turn it all over to Him; it is then that He says He will take care of us. In Him is where we find true peace that passes understanding, when we trade our own understanding for our Father's. The stories in this book demonstrate that. These true servants of God share how their lives were transformed when their understanding became the Father's. What a blessing to be a child of the King!"

— Missy Robertson, star of *Duck Dynasty*

"There is so much going on around us that we never see. Life is all about perspective, and when that lines up with the hand of God, it is remarkable to witness. This book and collection of stories from my friends at K-LOVE will inspire and encourage you greatly!"

— Andy Andrews, *New York Times* best-selling author, *The Noticer* and *The Traveler's Gift*

"Every day we all are faced with stress, situations we can't control and often the fear that we really are all alone. God clearly calls us to be *one body*. He wants us to come together—to tell our stories—to encourage and support each other. That is what these stories do—they give us courage in times of peril and strengthen us when we feel helpless. God has not left us alone—He is with us."

— TobyMac, top Christian artist and Grammy Award winner

"When my work started taking me to remote communities across Africa, Latin America, and Asia, I began hearing more and more about real miracles—God's intervention into the everyday on behalf of his people. For various reasons we in the West have forgotten how to see this evidence of God's hand on our lives—whether in big or small ways. In Don Jacobson's *It's a God Thing*, we are given the gift of a stirring collage of everyday miracles that encourage and inspire while also sensitizing us to the reality that God is still at work in incredible ways in our lives and around the world."

— Keith Wright, president, Food
for the Hungry

"*It's a God Thing* is a refreshing reminder of God's attention to the details of our lives. In a world that is often filled with an excess of bad news, the accounts of everyday miracles point to the bigness of God and the greatness of His mercy. My only complaint is that the book ended too soon!"

— Vicki Courtney, speaker and
best-selling author, *Your Girl,
TeenVirtue*, and *5 Conversations
You Must Have With Your
Daughter*

"Most of us, including myself, see miracles as something only happening during biblical times. Well, my friend, since the Bible applies today more than ever, I'd say we are still in biblical times, and miracles are very much alive and well! We've just gotten really good at explaining away miracles, no matter how big or small. My prayer is this book opens our eyes to the miracles that happen around us and even in our own lives. For me, the timing of this book is absolutely perfect. Sometimes I'm guilty of looking so hard for God that I miss Him right in front of me. May we all be reminded through *It's a God Thing* that some of the simplest moments in life can quite possibly be some of God's greatest miracles. Because of the cross, my very next breath is a *huge* miracle. Thank you, Jesus!"

— Bart Millard, lead singer of
MercyMe

"There is nothing better than hearing others talk about the ways that God has intervened in their lives. Miracles happen every day all around the world. These stories are incredible."

— Robert D. Smith, author,
20,000 Days and Counting

"Through everyday miracles discovered in the nooks and crannies of life, *It's a God Thing* presents a stunning glimpse of God through the lives of people like you and me. *It's a God Thing* is more than a book. It's an invitation, an encounter, a way of life. I recommend it highly."

— Stephan Bauman, president and
CEO, World Relief

"Nothing astonished people in the New Testament more than watching Jesus perform a miracle right before their eyes—and nothing inspires us today more than hearing He did it again! My good friend Don Jacobson, publisher of *The Prayer of Jabez*, has once again launched the perfect message for today—don't miss it!"

— Bruce Wilkinson, author, *The
Prayer of Jabez*

"This book is an unbelievable reminder of God's power and presence. These testimonies show how alive and active God is in our daily lives. Story upon story affirms to me that from the beginning to the end, God is with us and for us. Whether we are running out of a burning building, drowning, or need just a small whisper of encouragement, we can be confident that He will never leave us or forsake us. The ministry of K-LOVE and its listeners inspire me to be bold and courageous in sharing the love of Jesus."

— Michael McDowell, NASCAR
Sprint Cup Series driver

"God doesn't need for us to be aware of the miracles He's performing, but they're happening every day! *It's a God Thing*, a new book from K-LOVE, is a powerful vehicle to tell the story of a number of those miracles."

— Brandon Heath, 2008 New
Artist of the Year Dove Award
winner

it's a
GOD
thing

WHEN MIRACLES

HAPPEN TO EVERYDAY

PEOPLE

CREATED BY

DON JACOBSON AND K-LOVE

W PUBLISHING GROUP

AN IMPRINT OF THOMAS NELSON

Published in Nashville, Tennessee, by W Publishing, an imprint of Thomas Nelson.

Thomas Nelson titles may be purchased in bulk for educational, business, fund-raising, or sales promotional use. For information, please e-mail SpecialMarkets@ThomasNelson.com.

Scripture quotations marked NKJV are taken from the New King James Version®. © 1982 by Thomas Nelson, Inc. Used by permission. All rights reserved.

Scripture quotations marked NIV are taken from the Holy Bible, New International Version®, NIV®. © 1973, 1978, 1984, 2011 by Biblica, Inc.™ Used by permission of Zondervan. All rights reserved worldwide.

Scripture quotations marked NASB are taken from the New American Standard Bible®. © The Lockman Foundation 1960, 1962, 1963, 1968, 1971, 1972, 1973, 1975, 1977, 1995. Used by permission.

Scripture reference marked NLT is taken from the Holy Bible, New Living Translation. © 1996, 2004, 2007. Used by permission of Tyndale House Publishers, Inc., Wheaton, Illinois 60189. All rights reserved.

Library of Congress Control Number: 2013948791

ISBN 978-0-8499-2199-5

Printed in the United States of America

13 14 15 16 17 18 RRD 6 5 4 3 2 1

It's a God Thing is dedicated to the faithful listeners and supporters of K-LOVE.

Most of these stories are yours—thank you for your encouragement.

Contents

Contents

Acknowledgments

The family of God is an amazing group of people who every day sacrifice, share, and make meaningful connections in the pursuit of making Jesus known. The collective stories in a book such as *It's a God Thing* simply would not be possible without acknowledging, first, the amazing God whom we serve and, second, His people's willingness to share what God is doing in their lives.

So our heartfelt thanks to . . .

our great God and Savior, Jesus Christ—these stories begin and end with You

each of the authors whose stories appear in this first volume

Craig Borlase, the writer who helped our authors craft their stories

Acknowledgments

Christine Metcalf for her skillful editing

the W Publishing Group at Thomas Nelson—
partnering with you is a joy

the K-LOVE family, who each day affects millions of
listeners' lives for the gospel—our partnership with
you is a treasure

We are deeply grateful for each of you.

Introduction

You hear a lot of talk about miracles these days. Are they real? Skeptics will say that miracles are nothing but wishful fairy tales. Even some people who identify themselves as Christ-followers express doubts about them from time to time. For that matter, what exactly gets defined as a *miracle*?

There are certainly occurrences for many people that are, above all else, unexplainable. Whether it is a tumor that has suddenly disappeared from a medical scan, a near death experience, or simply unexpected provision that appears out of nowhere, many have been left with thankful hearts and few words to say other than, "It's a God thing."

These experiences are far more common than one may realize. We believe as you read the stories in *It's a God Thing*, you will come to believe that God really did and still does use His power and love to work for and on behalf of His people, His children. We hope you find fresh encouragement and joy as you read these testimonies, given by your brothers and sisters from around the world.

From almost fourteen hundred stories, we selected these forty-six to represent the ways in which God works in our lives, through His protection, provision, and physical and emotional healing. Some of the stories will make you say, "Wow! That's a miracle!" Others, perhaps not so dramatic, will help you begin to identify the more subtle ways in which God has worked or perhaps is working on your behalf even now to transform you into the image of His Son. We wanted to include those stories as well because they remind us that God's guidance is all around us, each and every day. In fact, perhaps the greatest miracle is the act of salvation that is available for all who sincerely seek it.

Please know that we are praying for you! And we look forward to hearing how God uses the stories in *It's a God Thing* to encourage you and make a difference in your life.

ONE

Escape

Brenda Jacobson

It is easy to love London. All that history, those theaters, the shops, and those winding lanes that weave their way back through time—it just seems magical. So when my son, Blair, graduated from high school and signed up for a term of study in England, I knew I wanted to accompany him on the trip over. Like any mother, I was going to miss him, and I wanted to be able to picture him more clearly in the months he was away. And what better place than London to create some lasting memories with him?

We wandered around Oxford and stood and stared at Stonehenge. We were amazed in the British Museum and goofed off outside Buckingham Palace. And then, on one of those rare but perfect English fall days, Blair got to do what he wanted to do most of all: find a secluded spot in a park and get lost in a great book.

That is how we ended up in Hyde Park.

"Are you sure you're okay?" I asked Blair.

"Mom, I'm fine," he said. "You're about to leave me in England for a whole semester. I think I can handle a couple of hours by myself."

"Just as long as you're sure. I'll meet you back here then, okay?"

"Okay. Bye, Mom."

I watched Blair walk away, book under his arm, so full of confidence. How did he grow up so fast? Where did my baby boy go? And how was I going to handle saying good-bye in a few days when I left him at school?

It was such a beautiful day that there seemed no point in feeling sad, so I decided to take a tip from Blair and find a secluded spot of my own, complete with gently rustling bushes and a peaceful bench, where I lay down, praying for him and soaking up the sun as well.

Only a few minutes had passed when a completely unrelated thought forced its way to the front of my mind: *Open your eyes.* I did exactly that, and as I blinked away the sunshine, I immediately noticed a man walking across the hill, directly toward me. He was tall and slender, dressed in muted colors that made him blend into the surroundings. He was about seventy-five feet away, and even though he was looking down, I had the sense that he was really troubled by something. His demeanor was a stark contrast to the serenity of the location, but that was not what bothered me. It was the three-foot length of bright-red rope that he was holding—each end was wound around his hands.

What possible use could he have for the rope? As quickly as this question entered my mind, I knew the answer; I looked to my side and noticed the bushes again. This time they did not look peaceful and inviting. If I was forced in there, nobody would be able to see or hear me. Whatever he was planning on doing, it wasn't good.

The man moved closer, now about fifty feet away, and another thought came to me: *Get up and walk quickly down the hill.* I did not feel any anxiety or panic or have sweaty palms or rapid breathing—nothing to indicate fear. I was simply calm as I obeyed these mental prompts. As I stepped away from the bench, I glanced over my shoulder. My movement startled the man, and he looked up. For just a moment, my eyes met his. They were chilling. Still, I felt no urge to panic, no impulse to run. I was just determined that I was not getting caught by him. I was going to get away.

I walked quickly for a minute and then looked back to see if he was following me. I couldn't see him anywhere, but what did that mean? Had he given up and gone away, or was he hiding somewhere else, waiting for a better time and place to grab me? I kept walking—projecting confidence just as those safety films tell you to—and made my way to the place where Blair and I had agreed to meet. I arrived and checked my watch. Not much time had passed since we said goodbye, and Blair would not arrive for another hour and a half. I really did not feel safe alone, so I headed straight back to the hotel. I was finished being an explorer for the day!

Our final days of the trip passed without incident, and I dropped Blair off at Capernwray. I flew home to Oregon, feeling the grief that visits every mother who leaves her child halfway around the world, completely beyond her protection. I found it easy to put the incident at the park out of my mind, but it came flooding back the moment I received a phone call from my friend Sheri Rose just a day or so after arriving home. She got straight to the point.

"Brenda, what happened to you while you were in England?"

"What do you mean?" I said, thinking of all the possible ways there were of answering her question.

"Last Wednesday the Lord woke me up to pray for you because you were about to be murdered."

I was stunned. We talked a little more and did the time calculations between the West Coast and England. It quickly became perfectly clear: God had awaken Sheri Rose at the exact moment I was alone in Hyde Park, lying on a secluded bench, while a man with a rope in his hands walked toward me. Could it be any clearer that God was protecting me?

Although all this happened a few years ago, I often think back to it. What I remember is not so much the man or the rope or the fear of what might have happened. What I remember is how God protected me. I now know that those words I heard were his voice, carried to me through the prayers of a friend.

TWO

A Provision of Friends

Kris Heckman

I believe that God knew my daughter would be taken from me so early on in her life. I believe he knew, and that is why the time we had together was so special. I believe he knew that from the moment I named her Micah, she would be more than just my daughter; she would be my friend.

Micah was such a special girl. Every parent says that, I know, but so much of what she did while she was alive still lives on in our hearts today. Her poetry and her journals are with us, and I never grew tired of hearing her pretty voice. Micah was a unique person, beautifully simple. When a boyfriend would come over, it was normal for her to show up at the door wearing sweatpants and a hoodie, her hair tossed up on her head as if she had just climbed out of bed. That was Micah—down-to-earth though sometimes opinionated, compassionate, and deeply caring about people. We all loved her greatly—me; her dad; her older brother, Jeremy; her family; and her friends.

The story around Micah's death is one that I always want to be remembered. It is a story that shows God's amazing love even in the most heartbreaking circumstances of life. It is a story about loss, but it is also a story about hope.

My husband and I were on the cruise of a lifetime to Alaska. On the third of July we departed from Seattle and met our eight tablemates at dinner that evening. Before the main course was served, one of them, a friendly guy named Mike, asked everyone to hold hands and say a prayer. As far as we could tell, we were the only other Christian couple at the table.

We did not get to talk at length to Mike and his wife, Elsie, until the next night. They told us about their prison ministry in New Mexico, and as our conversation flowed, the evening drew to a close and we were the only ones left in the dining room. We told them about our lives, about my husband searching for a new purpose in his work life. We told them about our two children, that Jeremy was twenty-one and Micah was eighteen. We asked them to especially keep our daughter in their prayers because she had just graduated early from high school and had moved to a small town in Nebraska where my husband's family lives. We told them that Micah now had her own apartment and was trying to figure out what to do next with her life.

I guess that was the point at which we realized that God had put us at the same table as Mike and Elsie for a reason. Mike told us that they were originally scheduled to go on a Christian cruise, but they felt the Lord leading them to our ship, the *Oosterdam*. They decided to follow what they were feeling and just asked God to put them at a table with people who needed them.

"I think you're the reason God put us here on this cruise," said Mike.

I was surprised by what he said, but I figured that we had the rest of the week to learn the deeper reason. Maybe they would be instrumental in helping my husband decide what to do with his life. Maybe their prayers for our daughter would really help.

The night ended, and we went to our staterooms. I fell asleep but woke again at 1:00 a.m. as the phone rang. It was my husband's brother from Nebraska. Micah had been in a car accident, and they were flying her to the medical center in Scottsbluff. Her heart had already stopped once.

We ran down to the main office and began the process of getting off the ship. We had just left Juneau and were on our way to the next port, and there was a six-hour period when our cell phones were useless. Almost immediately after we received the phone call, my husband asked the staff to please find Mike and Elsie. We knew nothing about them other than their first names and dinner table number. The staff found them, and when Elsie got to us, she was crying.

"Now I know why the Lord wanted us to be on this ship," she said. We had to agree, and we were so grateful that they both stayed with us and prayed while we waited for 9:00 a.m. to come around and the fishing boat to come alongside the ship. It paused just long enough for us to climb down a rope ladder and get on board, and then it took us to Yakutat, Alaska. From there we got on an Alaska Airlines jet to Anchorage, and while we were on the plane, we were given a snack tray. Neither of us felt like eating, but we could not help but notice that on the tray was a little card from the airlines with a picture of a sunset and the verse "Give thanks to the LORD, for he is good; his love endures forever" (Ps. 107:1 NIV). I just looked at my husband, knowing God was speaking to us.

Thirty-three agonizing hours after that first phone call, we finally made it to Micah's bedside. They kept her on life support until we got there, so we were able to kiss her and hold her and tell her how much we loved her. And then she left us and joined her Savior in heaven.

The hospital asked us to consider donating her organs, which we did. Later, at her wake, a friend from high school told us that during a unit in health class on organ donation, Micah had said she would definitely want to donate if she was ever in that situation. Hearing something like that helped us so much, as did knowing who Micah was a donor for: a sixty-three-year-old male, a fifty-two-year-old male, and a fifty-seven-year-old female. I have written to them all. We were able to meet the fifty-two-year-old, Micah's liver recipient, and he is doing well. Micah's left kidney recipient wrote back to tell us how he had become ill exactly one year before Micah died. He had been on a cruise when it happened, in Alaska, on a ship called the *Oosterdam*. He had required an emergency evacuation, just like us. We do not believe in coincidences. I am amazed at how God used him as one of the recipients, especially as he and his wife had also lost a child twenty years earlier in an accident. They knew how we felt.

Micah was such a huge part of our lives, and our hearts are still broken. But our faith remains strong. We believe in a God who loved us so much that he sent Mike and Elsie to us so we would not be alone when we first learned of Micah's accident. And we know that God's hand was mightily at work when, as the cruise carried on after we left, Mike and Elsie helped other couples at our table accept Jesus as their Savior. And we know God was at work in the lives of the two Muslim ship workers who helped us off the ship and who also came to faith as a result.

God works in ways we cannot even begin to comprehend. He has been so faithful, even in this heartbreaking time in our lives. We miss Micah so much and think of her constantly, but we also know that God is a great God. He gives eternal life to anyone who will confess he is a sinner and accepts salvation through the death and resurrection of his Son, Jesus. Our God, who placed the stars into space yet knows our names, calls his children home eventually. When it is our turn, we know that we will see Micah and never again have to say good-bye.

THREE

Jail Saved My Life and My Soul

Alison Wilson

We haven't met before, but you've seen me. You've quickened your pace while passing me on the sidewalk. You've tried to ignore me, but something about the sight of me hunched over in the doorway kept you from looking away. You've pulled your loved one close as our eyes met. Sometimes you smiled. Sometimes you didn't.

I might've been drunk, or I might've been high. I might've asked you for money, or I might've pretended you were not there at all. Like all homeless drug addicts, I lived for the moment—the moment when I no longer felt as though I was living. Being numb was the best I could hope for.

All that changed on April 20, 2011. Not that I knew it at the time. But as I stood, hands held behind my back, legs kicked apart, face forced down on the hood of the squad car, my life was about to change. My life was about to start all over again.

I don't know if I can remember the moment I became a drug addict—it's not as though you have an official enrollment date or anything—but I know I had been living on the streets since 2008, when my husband and I split up. By the time 2011 came around, I had to find a hundred dollars each day to keep me numb enough to get through the day. Mostly, I would get the money by stealing from anyone and everyone—stores included—but on April 20, I decided to go shoplifting somewhere new.

At that time my drug dealer wanted steaks. I don't know why, and I didn't question it. All I knew was that he wanted steaks and I wanted meth, so I found myself trying to secretly load about fifteen steaks into my bag in the grocery store. As I tried to walk out, the security guard caught me. And then things got ugly; with staff shouting at me and the security guard pushing me, I was only able to think about the meth I was missing out on.

For a drug addict the hardest part about going to jail is getting sober, and I hadn't been sober in more than ten years. My body was exhausted, and it was addicted, but that didn't make any difference to the police. I had been caught and was going to jail. My body would have to fix itself from behind bars.

And I was seven months pregnant at the time. I had taken so many drugs and abused my body so violently that the birth of my healthy baby boy two months later was another miracle all in itself. (He is thriving today, by the way.) But back in jail, I couldn't imagine ever getting out. Being pregnant meant being put in solitary confinement, locked down for twenty-three hours a day. I was allowed sixty minutes a day to shower and use the phones, but that was it. There were no outside privileges at all.

Not that any of that mattered to me at the start. For the first days I slept without eating, only getting up to use the bathroom. Every part of me ached, my stomach churned constantly, and as my body screamed at me for drugs, all I could do to numb the pain was dream about getting high. But even that was not enough. At times I would wake up—sometimes to darkness, sometimes to light—my body shivering with either hot or cold sweats. Like a child screaming for a toy it cannot have, my body went into a rage. There was nothing I could do but wait.

Sometime around the third day I woke up and, for a moment, felt better. The aches had subsided, and the sweats were gone. For the first time I was able to take a good look around me. The cell was super small and incredibly stinky. It had off-white walls, a cot with a gray blanket on it, and right next to it, a metal toilet and a Bible placed on the floor. No window; just some glass in the blue-colored metal door. By the time I finished looking around, panic had set in. I didn't want to be there. I didn't want to be there at all.

Now that I was sober and locked alone in my cell, one thing I had a lot of was time. I sat and reflected on what my life had become. The first real, undiluted thoughts that I had were about my two daughters. For the first time in years, drugs were not stopping me from missing them. For the first time in years, my heart ached because of what I had done to them. My sadness and shame were overwhelming. I had failed as a mother and as a human being. Looking at my life from the outside, I could reach only one conclusion: I hated what I saw.

Somehow, in the middle of all this, I had a moment of clarity. I could finally see my life for what it was. And what I saw was that it was totally out of control. I needed more help than simply getting sober to put it right.

It was the prison chaplain, Gary, who ended up helping me. He was younger than I expected and soft-spoken. He was real and down-to-earth, and I felt as if he would know whether a person was lying just by looking at her. I had lived as a drug addict for so long that lying was second nature to me; but as I started explaining my situation to him, I knew I needed to be nothing but honest. After I finished talking, he told me about Jesus, and I gave my life to the Lord. I returned to my tiny cell a changed woman. My heart was a million tons lighter. I was forgiven. I may have been locked up, but I was finally, gloriously, free.

I fell to my knees and poured my heart out to Jesus. For days on end it seemed as though all I did was pray, telling him about my regrets and my pains, about my worries and my hopes. I knew he was listening, and I knew he was answering all my prayers. For the first time in my life, I began reading the Bible, and as I did, that tiny cell didn't seem half as small.

I wanted to see the chaplain once more, and as we met again, I told him how I felt about my life. I told him that I wanted to change, but I did not know how that could happen. I had spent so long on the streets—could I really hope to change all that when I finally got out? I was terrified of what life would be like when I was released. My life had started again in jail, but it was still far too fragile and weak to be able to make it out there. How would I cope?

But there was another issue. My baby was nearly due, and if I stayed in jail, he would be taken away from me for sure. I felt caught. I needed help.

Gary told me that he ran some rehab classes and that he thought they would help me. I had done rehab before—and had walked out before the end every time. But this time, it might be different. He said that if I wanted to go to court and ask for the chance, he would come along with me and help plead my case.

When my court date finally came up, I was terrified. Gary had told me to pray, and he shared that passage from the Bible about how the birds do not worry about their next meal or where they will sleep. It helped a lot, but as I stood in front of the judge—whom I had met in the same courtroom before—I could feel the fear. I knew he didn't like me much, and as he asked me why I wanted to try rehab for the seventh time in my life, I stumbled over my words as I tried to explain what had happened and how desperate I was to go to a facility that would help me rebuild my life. The judge, unimpressed, just kept looking down at his desk. But then it was time for the chaplain to speak. When the judge asked him why he thought I should go to rehab at the taxpayers' expense, Gary stood up and filled the room with four words that I had not heard said about me in more than a decade.

"I believe in her."

I could not stop the tears, not then, and not when the judge granted me a stay at a live-in facility, where that very next day I began the next stage of my journey through recovery.

Over the next six months I watched my life get back on track. I learned how to control myself in potentially toxic situations, and I learned what my triggers were and how to stay away from them. I learned that while many of the life skills that I had acquired on the streets had kept me alive there, they were no use to me now. I learned healthy new skills for dealing with conflict, stress, and anxiety. Rehab helped me get my priorities straight and make goals for the future. And underpinning it all was my new personal relationship with Jesus, which gave me the strength to rebuild my life and see my dignity and self-confidence return like long-lost friends.

I graduated from the program in the fall. Just as the leaves were dying and winter was setting in, my life was finally returning to spring again. After too many years living far within my pain and self-pity, I was ready to reach out. I had become worthy of seeing my daughters again.

The moment I was reunited with my family was as sweet as any I have ever felt. I walked into the room, and there they were, with open arms and eyes full of tears. My daughters, who had been without their mother for so long, finally got the sober mother they deserved. And as I held them in my arms for the first time in years, I promised them that I would never leave again.

I could only make that promise—and I can only stick to it today—because of what God has done for me. I can do it only because I am free. And I am free only because one day I went to jail. There is not a day that goes by when I don't thank God for the events that began on April 20.

FOUR

Our Last Day Together

Sarah Forbes

They said it was going to be an epic snowstorm. The forecasters looked serious as they faced the camera and spoke of the next day as a mass of winds and whiteouts, warning of major disruption to travel plans and—*please, God, let it be mine*—school closures. Before the day was over, the word had spread: my school would close as well. My prayers were answered, and as a high school junior I felt nothing other than pure, unadulterated joy at the thought of missing a day in the classroom.

The next day I woke up expecting to see not much besides snow from my window. But there was none. None at all. The view looked the same as it had the previous morning. Same old grass, same old flowers, same old sidewalk.

What followed was a unique day. School was still canceled, so I spent the day with my mom, and for one special, beautiful series of moments, we were happy together. We laughed nonstop, talked about all kinds of crazy things, and just hung out the way two people do when they are both totally relaxed in each other's company.

It had not always been like this. For too long Mom and I had been arguing. Anything could trigger it, and it often did. I felt that she was never around enough and did not understand me. I felt disconnected from her as though her problems were so much larger than the boring day-to-day teenage problems. My mom had been sick for nearly my entire life, fighting infection and disease while enduring surgery after surgery. She had been through so much, and for that one day when the snow failed to show up, I was given a tangible demonstration of her love and devotion to me. For that one day, I had been able to open up to her.

As the day slipped into evening, I left for work, happy that the roads were clear, but happier that Mom and I had shared such a precious time together. When I returned five hours later, she was not there. She had been feeling sick and called the ambulance to take her to the hospital. The pneumonia she had been fighting since Christmas had turned into sepsis. By the time I arrived at her bedside, she had been put on a ventilator. A week later, she was dead.

In the seven years that have gone by since the snowstorm that never was and the beautiful, final day that Mom and I spent together, I have come to see just how present God has been during this time. Seemingly random encounters with people and events reinforced the message of his love and commitment to me, and I look back now with the clear knowledge of how much Mom truly sacrificed and loved me. I have grown into the young woman I am today because of her love and dedication, and I can never thank her enough for all she gave. It is a true miracle of God's mercy that I was given that day without snow, allowing me to begin my life without her while feeling thankful, loved, and known.

FIVE

Restored

Julie Kerrigan

They say that the dawn can come only after the darkest part of the night, but for me it felt as though this dark night was never ending. For years my husband and I had been praying that God would give us another child. It had taken us many years to conceive Gabrielle, our first, and the return to the pain and grief of infertility and miscarriages was painful to the extreme. We both had been broken. We both had been angry. We both had lost heart.

Somehow my spiritual temper tantrum blew over quicker than my husband's. After more than four years of trying for our second child, I was back in a place of surrender, desperate for God to intervene. For James, it was different. He is the type of guy who fixes whatever problem comes at him, and this was a problem he couldn't fix. After James had spent years believing that God would bring us another baby, my latest miscarriage had drained all hope and faith from him.

He felt angry and bitter toward God, and although he would still accompany us to church, he felt locked in his pain. He asked God to help him, but for James, it seemed as though God was on mute.

I had a plan to address his pain and bitterness that involved taking a beachside vacation and soaking in the beauty of God's creation. So that summer James, Gabrielle, and I flew to South Carolina. Our hotel was right on the beach, and I could not have anticipated a more glorious view from our window. The ocean was absolutely breathtaking, and I was sure this vacation would begin the healing in James's heart. But as we stood together on the beach, I sensed no change in James. He was emotionless, aloof. There was a darkness about him that he just couldn't shake. I missed my husband. I longed for the man of God I had married years ago.

After several days at the beach, we decided to take a trip to the aquarium. It was full, and every attraction was crowded, but we both enjoyed watching Gabrielle as she swam with stingrays, played with horseshoe crabs, and observed an array of ocean life. Her bright smile was enough to inspire our own, and when she begged us to take her to the Mermaid Boutique, we couldn't say no. Forty-five minutes and twenty photos later, she emerged, her face a picture of pure joy.

We were headed out, in search of the next attraction, when a woman who was standing against a wall leaned down and softly said to Gabrielle, "You are so beautiful."

Her compliment caught us off guard a bit, but James prompted Gabrielle to be polite, and she kindly said, "Thank you."

"You don't understand," the woman replied. "God thinks your heart is beautiful, and he has great plans for you!"

She carried on like this for a few seconds, telling Gabrielle directly about God's love for her. I wasn't sure what this woman's intentions were at first. It seemed as if she was purposely seeking us out. Why? Was she crazy? Did she want money? I decided to throw out a little test, so I looked down at my daughter and said, "Look, Gabrielle, she loves Jesus too!" When she replied that she did and that he was her Lord and Savior, I breathed a sigh of relief.

We said good-bye and continued to walk down the corridor. Then James stopped, told me that he was going back to speak with the woman, and disappeared. I will always remember the look in James's eyes as he spoke. It was one I had not seen in a long time. It was a look not just of desperation but of hope. As Gabrielle and I walked to the next exhibit, I wondered: *Could this woman be God's answer to our prayers?*

It only took a few minutes for James to find us. It looked as though he had been crying, which shocked me. For so long he had been in an emotional void—no tears but no real joy either. As he spoke, his voice sounded different too. He was animated again, not dull and flat like before.

"The woman wants to pray for you; she wants to pray for you now."

Somehow his words did not seem to have much effect on me. Instead, I was much more interested in what had gone on between the two of them. What had just happened back there? James told me that they had not said much. He explained that as we were walking away from her the first time, he just knew he had to go back and see her even though he could not explain it. As he had approached her, he thanked her for what she had said to Gabrielle and told her that the last year had been tough on us both.

Reaching out and holding his hand in hers, she just said, "I know."

With that touch, something miraculous happened. James said that he instantly felt a rush of something come over his body. Sorrow erupted within him, and he let out giant sobs. Through the tears he tried to breathe, and it took some time before he could say, "We have lost babies." That was when the woman encouraged him to bring me to her.

I guess I decided to go along with James to encourage him, not so much because I thought the woman was going to do anything with me. I was grateful enough that something looked as though it had shifted within him, and as we met her in the stairwell, she immediately started to pray. Just like my husband, I wept. For so long I had been hiding my pain, but in that moment I was powerless against it. Every hurt, every disappointment was stirred up within me, and I felt them all at once. I was trembling as I fell into her arms. After finishing her prayers, she looked directly into my eyes.

"The Enemy has been withholding things from you. It's not going to happen anymore."

As she turned to James, her voice changed. There was a note of authority as she spoke: "Now, Dad, you have played the victim for far too long. Jesus died and rose again to victory. You need to claim victory in that." As she spoke these words, she reached out and grabbed his hand. Immediately, James began sobbing again. I held my husband in my arms, him clinging to me for support, both of us weeping.

The woman started speaking about our troubles as if she had been through them all with us. She knew of our miscarriages, our plans of adoption, and even details of some of the most private moments in our grief. And she said that our babies who reside in heaven are beautiful. She said they were looking forward to meeting us.

Placing her hand on my stomach, she looked into my eyes. "You can continue pursuing adoption, but that is not his plan for you. Honey, you are with child." Those words never really registered with me. I had dismissed the idea of having any more children years before, but she just kept on repeating those words again and again. "You are with child." Still, I just didn't get it. Finally, turning to Gabrielle, she told her that she was going to be a big sister.

As we hugged good-bye, she told us she had not known why God had sent her to the aquarium that day, only that he wanted her to go there. Seeing how beautiful Gabrielle looked, and how broken James and I were, was all she needed to know what God's intentions were. Looking at me one last time, she smiled. "I will see you again someday."

We left without ever having asked her name.

In the hours and days that followed, James told me how the darkness that had occupied him for so long had now lifted. He said that he could see so much more clearly than he ever had before, and I could not have been more thankful. The Lord had answered my prayers.

But there was more to come even though I still could not see it. God had sent this woman not only for James but also for the both of us. Several days after meeting that woman, I finally understood it all. I was pregnant.

SIX

There Is Always Hope

Tiffany Matthews

My senior year had just begun, and I was driving to school. I do not remember everything that happened, other than the rain and the brakes and my leaving the road and getting T-boned by the other driver. But I know that for my mother, who had left the house just a few minutes after me, the sight of her daughter's car crushed like a tin can and on the wrong side of the road was enough to make her hysterical.

She got to me before the ambulance crew did, but she did not need a doctor to tell her that I was in trouble. My 2001 black Toyota Celica looked as though an angry giant had picked it up and hurled it down to the ground. By the time I had been cut free and rushed to Baptist Hospital, the verdict was clear: I was in a coma.

I did not know it at the time, but as soon as I arrived at the hospital, I was wheeled from one machine to the next, where CT scans and MRIs tried to piece together the jigsaw that would tell the doctors what was wrong with me. Eventually the evidence was clear, and I was diagnosed with a diffuse axonal traumatic brain injury. What did that mean? It meant that my whole brain had been impacted, not just a small part. Every part of it was bruised; I was in trouble.

My parents listened as the doctors told them that more than 90 percent of people with severe diffuse axonal traumatic brain injury never wake up. If I was one of the lucky ones and did manage to regain consciousness, the doctors could not be sure about what kind of life I could hope to lead. Best-case scenario? What was left of my young life would be spent in a nursing home, dependent on help for everything. I would spend my days in a vegetative state until, one day, some infection or other underlying condition would steal away what little life I had left.

My parents and friends had no doubt as to how serious my condition was. It was clear that with so little hope from the medical staff, there was only one option left open to them: hold on tighter than ever to their belief that God could heal me. In a situation as dark and fearful as any they had experienced, they had to remind themselves and others that only God is in control. They could do nothing else but pray.

Prayer chains started up on Facebook, and T-shirts were made to get my story out. Thousands of prayers were offered up, and a surging tidal wave of faith swept me up with it. And then, on the eighth day after the accident, I woke up.

I do not remember anything at all about the day I opened my eyes. It was as if my brain was wiped clean. My first memories of my new life are in the rehabilitation center, but even those are only vague shadows of recollections. There were tears, kind nurses, and therapists, but I do not recall much else.

And for the first six weeks, I did not speak a word; I was locked in silence.

The journey back to full health was a long one; I had to learn how to walk, talk, eat, and take care of myself all over again. I went to sleep a high school senior and woke up a baby. But with lots of therapy, including speech, physical, occupational, and recreational, I got it all back. And so, on December 22, 2011, seventy-one days after the accident, I was discharged from the hospital.

In the days before I left, the staff at the hospital tried their best to prepare me for what life would be like once I was home—especially at school. They told me that school was going to be very different, and their cautious attitudes and concerned eyes told me they did not think I would be able to do it. They admitted that my recovery had been rapid and amazing, but I had to be realistic. I had to know my limits.

Well, I guess I kind of listened to them. I was realistic, and I did expect there to be limits—but only those set by God himself. He had brought me this far, and I had faith enough to believe that it was for a purpose. And I did not believe that he was giving up on me.

So maybe that is why I wasn't surprised that six months after I left the hospital, I stood in my blue cap and gown at Calvary Baptist Church, alongside my classmates, ready to graduate on time. My setback had been huge, but God's rescue had been even greater. That following August, I started my freshman year of college (on time, of course!), and I even made the dean's list.

Today as I'm writing this, I'm finishing up my first year of college, and I already know how my accident and miraculous healing have changed me. Having spent so much time in physical therapy, I know what it is like to battle discouragement and fear, so now I feel called to change my career path from nursing to physical therapy.

But there is more to it than that. This whole accident has taught me the greatest lesson of all: to better appreciate the life-changing truth that God is alive! I have learned not to take my precious time here on earth for granted. Am I ready to give account of what I have done here on earth? Am I using what little mustard seed of faith I have to serve my God? Does my life bring God glory?

This is where all our stories begin—in the place where we surrender to God, allowing ourselves to be rescued by him and choosing to live with all the passion and all the courage and all the faith we can lay our hands and hearts on. That is where life begins—even when we are moments away from death.

SEVEN

A Message from Heaven

Debra Smith

I don't ever remember Thanksgiving falling on my father's birthday, and five months after he died, I found myself anticipating the holiday with a bittersweet blend of emotions.

I had tried to keep busy, but the truth is, I was sad.

I was sad because I still loved my father just as much as I had when he had been alive. I loved him, and I missed him. I missed his smile, his sense of humor, his laugh, his hugs, his companionship. Most of all, I missed him loving me back.

This deep, heavy grief lasted for several weeks. I was tired of feeling it, but nothing could shake it. Not even busyness. I had unlocked the door, and there was no way that grief was going to leave.

One night I lay down on my bed with my daughter, Sarah. It was near her bedtime, and I was preparing to read to her from a book I had found while sorting through my parents' belongings. It was an old book, one my mother read to me as a child—*The Little Engine That Could*, written by Watty Piper. It tells the story of a smaller, weaker engine overcoming the scorn of the bigger engines. It is about perseverance, positive thinking, and trust, and the moment I found it, I had been reminded of how happy I was as a child when my dear mother read it to my brother and me while snuggling up together in bed with her. With Sarah beside me and the book in my hand, it felt good to be re-creating such a happy scene.

Before I continue, there is something you should know about my dad. He had the most distinctive way of signing cards and notes. It was not just his penmanship; it was his choice of words. He had a special way of referring to himself, always signing his cards to those he loved, "Love, The Me." He was "The Me." I don't know why, but he just was. It was one of the many things that made him so great, another example of his unique signature style on life.

As Sarah and I read, we reached the middle of the story, with the little engine feeling dejected and overlooked. I turned a page and watched in wonder as a small, raggedy piece of paper floated down from the book, landing gently on my chest. At first I felt inquisitive, but that soon gave way to feeling dumbfounded and overwhelmed. I picked up the little paper and drank those three words in, taking them down deep into my weary soul.

Love, The Me.

It was simple and succinct, profound and poignant. It was all I needed, and it left me awestruck.

Of course I could use logic to explain it all, but that would be like trying to define a kiss in terms of mathematical angles and chemical exchanges. I took the note to heart in the same way that it had floated onto my chest—unexpected, welcoming, open. When I needed to know my dad's love, I got it. In that moment, I knew with an assurance greater than my grief that my heavenly Father loved me, just as I knew that my earthly father had. I knew it, and it changed me.

Perhaps it is not great theology, but I think you can summarize the whole Bible with my dad's three little words, *Love, The Me.*

EIGHT

My God Coma

David Spencer

People who like to get high know which room to watch in a party. Not the one with the music and not the one with the food. But the one with the bright lights and the lockable door.

I was watching the bathroom. I guess I must have been twenty at the time, and I had been getting high for enough years to know that from the number of people going in and out of the room, there was something good happening on the other side of the door. So I waited my turn to have some fun.

My story with drugs began when I was fourteen. I started smoking pot and doing trippy drugs during my freshman year of high school. I played around with *fun* drugs but never did any *serious* drugs. By the time I was twenty, I had moved on to coke. During those school years, my drug use never seemed to be a problem. It was kind of like a weekend hobby. I took the drugs, but they didn't take me.

Well, all that changed the moment I decided to go inside

that bathroom and see what was going on for myself. I walked in, nodded to the guy holding the straw, leaned over, and took a huge snort. I thought it was just another line of coke. Turned out I was wrong, and six hours later I was still high. And I mean really high. It wasn't coke; this was crank—a powdered form of methamphetamine.

And so began my addiction even though I didn't believe it at first. Despite having grown up in a strong Christian family and being heavily involved with church all my life, I liked to party . . . and I partied hard. In those early months that followed my introduction to meth, I still considered myself to be just another weekend warrior. I'd start out on Friday night and then come down on Sunday morning, ready to get back to work the next day. But it was only a matter of time before it got out of control. One day, midweek, I broke my weekend-only rule and got high.

For two years I rode the downward spiral, allowing my meth addiction to draw me into the dark life of the underworld. I was stabbed. I was shot. I had all my upper teeth bashed out of my mouth, and I became a debt collector for some of my drug dealers. I didn't care what happened to me, and I didn't care what I did to others. I was a very good debt collector.

It wasn't just strangers that I hurt. During that time, I stole from my church, from my family, and from anyone who trusted me enough to leave me alone for five minutes. I was a full-blown addict, devoting every breath to getting more drugs.

Along with the highs there were the lows. I would wake up after a four-day bender feeling as though I wanted to die. I had become the worst version of myself.

Thankfully God was not through with me. He used a few tricks to give me the wake-up call I needed. First, my parents finally realized I was doing drugs. Even though I had been living with them, I had managed to hide the full extent of my drug use. But once they discovered the whole truth—the meth, the crime, the depths to which I had crawled—they told me that enough was enough. They were going to kick me out of their house.

That hit me hard. Realizing that the only two people who loved me, no matter what, didn't want to be around me anymore—well, that hurt.

Soon after, I became really sick. I had somehow gotten massively dehydrated and ended up hospitalized for two days. It was the break I needed even though I left the hospital with the intention of getting high as soon as I possibly could. I made my way over to my meth hut, where I knew there would be enough meth for me to get the escape from reality my body was craving.

As I sat there, I looked around me. I looked at the other people in the house. They were older than me, and they looked as though they were dying from the inside out. And that's when I finally realized that I didn't want to be like these guys. I wanted more from life.

Nobody really noticed as I left. I made it back to my room in my parents' house and fell to my knees. I cried out to Jesus to take all this away from me. I don't know whether it was a hallucination from the lack of sleep or whether I actually did hear God's voice speak to me, but whatever the cause, I suddenly knew God was listening to me. He was going to get me out of this mess. Strange as it sounded, I knew he needed just one week.

I asked my parents to let me stay in the house for a while longer. I told them that things would be different at the end of a week, that God was going to help. They agreed, and for the next seven days I slept, ate, and went back to sleep. I call that week my God coma.

Ten years later I am writing these words clean and sober. I have not touched drugs since, and I now know that the only thing worth living for is Christ. I have an amazing wife, a beautiful son, and an addiction ministry at my church. We help people dealing with addiction find mentors to help keep them accountable. Indeed, with God all things are possible.

NINE

The Unlikely Ballerina

Lauri Khodabandehloo

"What are we doing today, Mom?"

It was a good question. I had been asking it myself since waking up. Lying there in the Saturday morning silence, I had wondered how my daughter and I would pass the time that lay ahead of us. All I knew was that doing nothing at all was not an option.

In the twelve years that had passed since the birth of Farema, my youngest of four daughters, I had grown used to life being a little bumpier than it had been before. She is a precious jewel of a child, with aqua eyes that have sparkled from the very moment she was born. But even from the start she was so different from her sisters that it seemed she was from another world.

Like any mother, I knew I needed to listen to my instincts. Holding her was such a different experience than holding her sisters when they were infants, and it didn't take me long after her birth to begin reading books in the city library about childhood disorders and syndromes. By the time Farema was a few weeks old, I had already learned more than I wanted to know, and years before the professionals would diagnose my child with classic autism, I had already figured it out.

And there she was, with ringlets of light golden brown hair that giggled down past her tiny shoulders, nearly reaching her waist, looking at me for the answer to the riddle of the day. And me in my robe, sitting at the kitchen counter, cradling a coffee, and looking into those mysteriously beautiful eyes of hers. What were we going to do today?

With Farema each day's activities were encountered at the same breakneck speed. She would start the morning running and keep on going until exhaustion finally forced her to fall into bed at night. My challenge that Saturday was to find something suitable. There were not many options open to us.

But that could wait, just a little. First I wanted to reply to her question with a hug.

"Well, good morning, baby!" I smiled at her, bending close to wrap my arms around her. Not too tight and not too long, but just brief enough. With Farema, hugs did not last long unless she initiated them; on those rare occasions, my joy would light me up for hours. Her sisters had always been the huggy-lovey types, but Farema was different. Her shows of physical affection were rare and precious jewels.

It was one of those windy October mornings that often bring a little sun, a little cloud, and a little rain to Oregon's Willamette Valley. Bike riding was out of the question—but not because Farema would dislike it. I was more of a dry-weather biker than I had been in my younger days, and my recent hip replacement placed limits on my activities. Staying in and letting our imaginations fly with a craft project were out of the equation too. Farema had to be moving—flying, if at all possible—from morning to bedtime.

With all my other daughters married and living in their own homes, weekends often threw up this kind of search. Yet somehow, today felt different. Somehow, not having a plan felt like the right kind of plan to have.

"Let's get dressed and go for a drive, and maybe I'll think of something we haven't done in a long time, okay?"

Farema flew into her jeans and sweatshirt, raced into her shoes, and was ready to go.

Driving toward downtown, we turned down Thirteenth Avenue and pulled up to a stoplight in front of the city ice-skating rink. I had not been to this part of town for a long time, and it kind of surprised me to see the rink there. I had forgotten our city had one, but as we sat at the light, I turned to my daughter.

"Hey, Freem, there's the ice rink! Want to go watch the skaters just for fun?"

A girl of few words, she just smiled back. That was enough.

Between the crazy noise blasting out across the echoing arena and the surging crowd of people all blurring before our eyes as they skated round and round, I thought this would be a short visit. But then I looked down and saw Farema's face, illuminated with excitement, alive with delight. I wondered, *Would Farema be interested in giving it a try too?*

Even as the words flowed easily out of my mouth, I could hardly believe I was asking her: "Baby, do you want to try it?"

Farema's head nodded in eager agreement, and her hand reached out for mine, pulling me speedily toward the cashier. She would have to go alone, as my hip wasn't going to let me get out there, but the skate guard assured me that kids younger than mine often skated alone the first time.

"We have guards on the ice to give her a hand as well," she said, "and I'll show her how to tuck and roll if she thinks she might fall. She'll do fine!"

Once I walked Farema down the steps to the edge of the rink—she taking Bambi steps and me offering up silent prayers for the Lord to keep her safe—I let go. The second her blades hit the ice, she was gone. No looking back, no acknowledgment of my advice to keep holding on to the side and watch out for the other skaters. She was gone, and all I could do was watch.

I finally moved out of the way of a crowd of other skaters trying to pass me to join Farema on the ice, and I climbed up the concrete steps to the viewing area. And there, perched on a wooden bench behind huge plateglass windows, I saw it happen.

Within minutes Farema let go of the wall, carefully entering the flow of skaters who swept their way around the rink. Some were big, others small, but the size did not seem to determine whether they wobbled or glided, staggered or soared. Some other gravity was at work on them, and by the time she had finished one full circle of the rink, Farema sped up and moved in toward the center of the huge rink, where the more advanced skaters were practicing jumps and spins.

I held my breath, transfixed by what I was seeing. The woman sitting behind me leaned forward to ask me whether that young girl with the flowing hair was mine, and how long had she been skating to get that good.

With tears falling down my cheeks, I found it difficult to answer her, but eventually the words came out: "She just started."

The more I watched, the more I could feel a presence, something mysterious yet tangible around me that I had not felt when I first sat down. It stayed with me, growing and forming until I knew a little of what it was: an overwhelming peace that filled my heart and soul with the knowledge that God could see this, too, that he was watching and protecting this child of mine—and his.

From that day forward Farema became a fixture at the rink. She went on to compete and perform and make friends we would never forget. So much happiness and hope came from that one spontaneous, dangerous, and unexpected Saturday morning.

And that tangible sense of God standing with me, watching out for his daughter . . . it never really left me. No matter what curves life throws us, I know today as I knew then that we never travel that road alone. God is with us to the very end.

TEN

Surprised by Hope

Amy Ward

"Today is your six-month birthday, little man. Or it would have been . . ."

I sit on the floor of my living room, looking at outfits that have never been worn, talking to the son I have never held. He died inside me almost a year ago, but it has taken me this long to get around to packing up all those newborn clothes.

At first I did not want to get rid of all the things we had bought. Each item had been brought back home with so much excitement and hope, and keeping them was my way of holding on. Lord knows how I needed some hope back then. But gradually, as time moved on, I have been able to let go and step away from the clothes. They moved farther back into the closet and then from my house to my mother's garage. Slowly, I have been saying good-bye.

Here among the piles of shop-perfect outfits and clear plastic boxes I can see that there is no point in keeping them. No point at all. Besides, these aren't the first set of clothes that have left the house in the last year. Perhaps I'm getting used to it?

As well as feeling ready to let go, I know that these unworn outfits have the potential to do good—more good than they can sitting here, at least. When my mom—an investigator for Children, Youth, and Families—called me to say she knew of a woman who was looking after her six-month-old grandson, I liked the idea of handing them over. My son will not be wearing them, but at least someone will.

The loss of my son is not the only pain I have endured. I have grown accustomed to life being painful. Literally. I have been living with rheumatoid arthritis since I was twenty-two— beginning a month after giving birth to my daughter—but in order for the fertility medication to work and provide a little brother or sister for our beautiful eight-year-old daughter, I needed to go off my regular medications. That meant a return of the pain that robbed me of almost all my independence. It meant that I could barely take care of myself, let alone look after my daughter or husband. I needed help with everything from getting dressed to brushing my hair.

For an independent person such as myself, this was about as difficult a time as I had ever experienced. But if it meant we could have another child, no sacrifice was too great.

A week after I lost my baby, my husband told me he did not want to be my husband any longer. He said he had met someone else.

What followed was the very worst type of pain I have ever experienced. Between losing the baby and going through the divorce, there were times when I felt as though my world were crumbling away. And yet, even though I was losing so much of myself—no longer could I define myself as a pregnant woman, as a mother-to-be, as a wife—something inside me felt peaceful. Somehow, I had a feeling that God was guiding every step.

So here I sit, alone on the floor, preparing to give away the clothes my unborn son never got to wear. And in spite of everything that has gone before, I feel at peace. I really do.

That was two years ago. I was ready for a clean break and a fresh start, not to forget about the past but to move on to whatever was waiting for me and my daughter in the future. And I have. I found out that I could no longer have children and had to undergo a hysterectomy, but it did not overwhelm or shake me to the core. I knew that I could still be a spiritual parent to the youth in my life, and I felt that it was right for me to become a foster mom. I wanted to give children a safe, loving environment, if only for a night. I also wanted to mentor families, helping them better care for the children who came into my custody.

So, more than a year ago, I became a licensed foster parent, and just a few months after that, I received a call from Children, Youth, and Families. They told me that they had a twenty-one-month-old boy and a five-month-old little girl they had just taken into custody. They wanted to know if I could take them in, if only for a short time. That old feeling of God being at work returned, and as I headed to the office to pick them up, my heart started jumping.

Before I even saw them, I knew without a doubt that their

stories and my story were about to be woven together by God himself.

He was sitting on the floor of the social worker's office, playing with trucks and books. He looked uncared for, with shaggy, dirty-blond hair; a long-sleeved striped polo shirt; navy pants; and black tennis shoes. But he had the most beautiful eyes I had ever seen: a mix of green and hazel but too sad and dull for a child of that age.

The baby girl was asleep in the arms of one of the social workers in the office. She was the baldest baby I had ever seen, and yet I was shocked at how much she resembled me when I was a baby. She was as cute as could be, and I loved her from that very first moment.

I was giddy with God-soaked excitement and wanted to share the news with my mom. She still worked in the department, so once the meeting with the social workers was over, the three of us made our way down the hall to her office.

We sat and talked for a while. My mom wanted to know what I could tell her about the children, and as I told her what I knew of their history—about the difficult start they had both had to their lives—my mom's face suddenly changed.

"What is it?" I asked.

"You remember the six-month-old boy being looked after by his grandmother? The one you gave the clothes to?"

"Yes . . . ," I said, my heart already surging and leaping from within me.

"Well, you're holding him right now. He's the boy, the same one."

She was right. Somehow God had brought into my care the very same boy to whom all those clothes had gone. God had gone before me, even enabling me to provide for my future child when I felt as though I had lost so much of my future. Though I did not see it at all—not until the very moment that the tapestry was revealed—God was working away from view, weaving the threads of our lives together. He is the one who knits all of us together in our mothers' wombs, and I know he knitted both of these babies for me!

A year ago I formally adopted these two wonderful children, and today, as a single mom of three, I count myself abundantly blessed beyond even my wildest dreams. How great is our God, people? How great indeed!

ELEVEN

Does God Watch Baseball?

Donald L. Jacobson Sr.

"We're going to a ball game!"

These are good words for any man to say to a son. They were especially sweet to me when I saw my son's eyes light up with excitement. Donnie had played Little League baseball, and this would be his first time attending a professional game. With his twelfth birthday coming up, I hoped the outing would be an event we would both remember. But, as so often happens, God's plans were even bigger than my own.

We were living in Portland, and I was working for Bell Telephone Company as an installer. Week in, week out, I put in the hours, and my sixty-five-dollar-a-week paycheck was just enough to keep a roof over our heads and food on the table for our family of six. We weren't poor, but we weren't rich, and from time to time the money pressures felt a little heavier than they should for a man with a job like mine.

This was 1967, but things were not so different back then.

Like all twelve-year-old boys, Donnie was both a big child and a little man, just like me. We arrived at the game early, crossed the stadium parking lot, and walked in under the great archway to the home of the Portland Beavers. Donnie's wide eyes were looking everywhere. Neither of us wanted to miss a thing.

We took our seats in the left field bleachers, down along the left field foul pole, and settled in to watch the batting and infield practice. We looked out at the Beavers and talked about our favorite player, Ray Fosse. He was twenty years old at the time, six feet two and 215 pounds. He was the kind of player who gets twelve-year-old boys dreaming about playing ball.

The hours passed quickly. Both of us were busy commenting on everything that went on below. For once in our lives, we were the same age, he and me.

In time, the real game started. The scores were marked and the bats swung. At some point in the early innings, a player struck a pitch with such grace and power that it sailed right up over the outfield and into the right field bleachers. Donnie and I watched the small crowd of people scramble for the ball until a young man rose up, ball held high in triumph. He had gained his trophy and had the smile to prove it. Donnie said nothing, but I knew what he was thinking because everyone else in the stadium was thinking the same thing.

I decided on a whim to turn my thought into a prayer, flinging out a short, silent request: *Lord, it would sure be nice if I could get a baseball for my boy.*

Looking up, I caught sight of the Beavers' catcher, Ray Fosse, stepping up to bat. Ray would go on to become a major-league player, but he was then playing with the Beavers. Ray stood out; he always did. When he was catching, he would always stand his ground and take whatever hits came his way. He was the one to watch.

He shuffled a bit, looked at the pitcher, and froze in a ready stance. The ball came straight at him, clean and fast. We heard the crack of his bat, and all eyes leaped into the air, spotting it far above in the sky. It sailed a long, long way before I realized it was coming straight toward me. Barely having any time to think, I raised my hand to knock it down and saw it fall right below my feet. A shuffle occurred as hands scrambled to reach it. Quickly ducking down, I felt for the ball. Instantly my fingers found it and held on tight as I stood up tall, handing it to Donnie.

We almost couldn't believe what had happened. His own baseball, hit by Ray Fosse! Out of those thousands of baseball spectators, out of the hundreds sitting in the cheap seats, we were the ones holding the ball!

Donnie was still holding tightly to the ball the next day when he and I returned to Civic Stadium and the scene of our moment of triumph. Through the chain-link fence that surrounded the practice cages, we could see Ray, swinging that bat with all the power and fury he had unleashed the previous day. As he was getting ready to pack up and leave, Donnie and I called out to him—like the two big kids we both were—and asked him to sign our ball. He did, and Donnie and I went home with smiles every bit as wide as they had been the day before.

I have experienced many miracles in my life. I have known them during my military service, while doing missionary work, or flying as a bush pilot. I know what it is to fly through clouds and a storm and know the hands of God are underneath, holding me safe. I have felt them before, real as life itself. But this, this was different. It was a small thing, but it was a miracle—of that I am sure. Miracles are not always big. Sometimes the small ones shout the loudest of God's love and care for each of us. Even today, almost half a century later, I am still grateful to God for answering my prayer that day.

TWELVE

Choosing to Obey

Michelle Myre

Most of the time we choose to believe that many of the miracles that happened so long ago are no longer repeated today. We might pray for God to help us with smaller things—the job searches, the flight caught up in turbulence, the pain or grief. But what about the larger things? What about the blind and the dead? Doesn't God still want us to rely on him for their healing too? Sometimes it is not just faith that we need. It is courage as well.

My daughter and I were driving to the grocery store one hot afternoon. It must have been almost one hundred degrees, and all of us Northwest folks were struggling. Even so, when I saw a young woman lying on her back on the black asphalt of a school parking lot, something felt wrong to me. That did not seem like a good way to get a suntan, and on instinct I felt compelled to turn into the parking lot.

I pulled up beside a beat-up old truck and walked over to

the girl. She was either still a teen or just in her early twenties, and she lay with her long blonde hair and white dress spread out on the asphalt. An older lady was bent over the girl and talking on the phone. I asked her if she had called 911, but she just looked at me and said that she just wanted to see why this girl was sleeping on the ground. I was not impressed and told her to hang up and call 911 right away.

Then someone else joined us, appearing out of the truck. I guessed that he was the boyfriend, for as he saw the girl, he started sobbing and screaming her name, telling her to wake up. He was shaking her, grabbing her by the shoulders, and shouting. Whatever he thought he was doing, it wasn't going to do much good. She needed CPR right away.

I made him lay her down and strong-armed him away. I told him that if he wanted her to live, he needed to let me see what was wrong with her. As soon as I got down beside her, I could tell that she was not breathing and was in very bad shape. Her pulse was racing at more than two hundred beats per minute, and I could see her heart pounding in her chest. We were running out of time.

Out of nowhere a retired firefighter showed up. I was so grateful for his help, and immediately we started the resuscitation process together. Hands on top of each other, directly on the breastbone, arms straight, me administering fifteen compressions before he administered the two rescue breaths. We worked to a steady rhythm, just as we had been trained.

After seven or eight full rounds, the young girl's gray face told the story of impending death. Sweat was pouring down both our faces as the sun beat down, my knees were burning up from the hot asphalt, and I was frantic to save her. Each time I pressed down on her chest, her body made a horrible wheezing sound as breath was forcibly pushed out by my hands. I was scared that this was how it was going to end. I realized that what we were doing with human hands just wasn't working.

Mr. Retired Firefighter was looking at me expectantly. It was my turn to deliver the compressions, but instead, I heard a voice audibly whisper into my right ear: *Pray.*

Nothing else. Just a quiet, commanding voice. *Pray.*

By this time I had the sense that quite a crowd had amassed around us, maybe ten or fifteen people. For a split second I thought, *What will these people think of me when I do this?* But I chose to obey and step out in faith. With my hands poised over her chest to do compressions, I placed them gently on her and spoke the words that came to me: "Breathe! In Jesus' name!"

There was no pause, no time lag, no period where we sat and waited and wondered what was going to happen or what we should try next. As soon as the prayer left my lips, the girl's body immediately convulsed upward as though a giant hook had yanked her up toward heaven. She opened her eyes and took in a tremendous gulp of air—the kind a diver would take after returning to the surface. She drank it in, filling every part of her body with fresh air. It was the sweetest music my ears had ever heard.

"Where am I?" she asked.

My heart was overjoyed, and as I sat back on my heels, exhausted and exhilarated at the same time, I told her that she would be okay. She fell back into the firefighter's arms, and within a minute the paramedics arrived and took over.

As I stepped back, with tears flowing down my face, my

spirit was rejoicing. I couldn't stop myself from praising Jesus. "Did you see that? God saved her! That was awesome! Thank you, Jesus!" People were more focused on the paramedics as they gave her oxygen and continued to stabilize her. Someone in the crowd called back to me, "Oh yeah, sure."

No doubt, to some of the observers, I looked like a looney tune, praising Jesus like that, but the strange looks did not bother me. I was a little sad that I couldn't find the retired firefighter, though. I wanted to thank him, but he had vanished. Who knows where he went next?

I left soon after too. Maybe not everyone knew what really happened to that woman. But I did. I knew. And so did my daughter, who watched it all from the van. We drove away, both amazed and humbled by the fact that by holding my hand and whispering in my ear, God led me right up to the front row of a beautiful miracle.

Miracles do not get replaced by advances in technology. They are not just stories stuck in Bible times. They are still happening today. Sometimes we just need to be obedient enough to believe it.

THIRTEEN

One Last Scan

Chanda Miller

This looks like a pregnancy that started to grow and then ceased to do so. You can wait for the tissue to pass, or we can use medication to hasten a miscarriage, or we can schedule a D & C (dilation and curettage).

The e-mail was as brief and brutal as the news it contained. In just a few words it confirmed what one nurse practitioner and one doctor had already told me—at nine weeks, my pregnancy was over. They said it was not "viable," but I preferred to use other words. The child who was being knitted together in my womb was dead.

It had started a few days earlier when I experienced sudden bleeding. In the first few minutes of the ultrasound that followed, I moved from cautious hope to complete despair, watching the nurse practitioner as she struggled to find not just a heartbeat but a baby. The doctor was called in for a second opinion, and both agreed that the worst had probably happened. I did all that I could do—the only thing I could do—and placed this child at God's feet. Whatever happened, I wanted his will to be done.

More tests followed, and whatever optimism they threw up was quickly quashed. Within a week of my first ultrasound, I was reading an e-mail that informed me of my choices: wait for the tissue to pass, kick-start a miscarriage, or have the doctor take out the tissue. It seemed as though no time had passed, and this child of mine suddenly had lost it all, even the right to be called "baby." Now he or she was simply "the tissue." It made me weep even harder.

I decided to do the one thing I could for my baby: wait until my body did what it should do naturally. I found that the Holy Spirit was giving me the strength to praise the Lord in the face of this trial, but after nine days of nothing happening, and a second ultrasound with yet another doctor, I gradually began to feel peace about scheduling the D & C.

With my husband at my side and a wonderful nurse guiding me through the process, I entered pre-op. These two were my pillars of encouragement, but through it all my firm foundation was God himself. I knew then, as I know now, that all things work together for good for those who love the Lord and are called according to his purpose. I knew that God only ever intended good for me—even in the death of my child. And I knew that my baby was safe in his loving arms.

Before starting the procedure, the doctor scheduled to carry out the operation had some questions for me. He was puzzled by the fact that not one of the three people who had conducted my ultrasounds had been able to find any baby at all. And he was concerned that one of my tests had shown abnormally high hormone levels. He thought I could be experiencing one of three things: a molar pregnancy—an abnormal growth of tissue that can potentially lead to uterine cancer—or a partial molar pregnancy or multiple cysts on my ovaries that were mimicking a healthy pregnancy. He wanted to make me aware of the situation as he saw it, and he wanted to have a look for himself with another ultrasound before taking me into the operating room.

I was shocked by what he told me, but I remained confident that my God was in charge. As they wheeled me down on my hospital gurney to the imaging department, I reminded myself that I had been able to trust him with my baby, and I could trust him with myself.

I was used to the silence that hung in the air as technicians scanned my empty womb. But on this occasion the silence did not last long. "Well, there's the baby . . ."

I felt the relief flood into me, filling me up and banishing the anxiety about cysts and molar pregnancies and uterine cancer. At least we could proceed with the D & C, and I could properly grieve this little life that had started and finished within me.

"Ahh! And it looks like it has a nice heartbeat. It's moving around real good in there."

I cannot describe the feelings. Shock. Awe. Disbelief. Joy. I could hear myself shouting, "Praise God! Praise God!" and within seconds I was watching on the screen my healthy eleven-week-old baby kick his little feet and swing his little arms.

"Do you want to hear the heartbeat?"

The tears were beyond my control as the room filled with the sound of my baby's heart racing along. The heart that nobody could find in the baby that people had said was long gone. There was life within me, not death.

Later, talking to the doctor, realizing how close I had come to terminating what was in fact a healthy baby, I touched his arm and told him that I thanked God for giving him the wisdom to be thorough and diligent. His reply was confirmation that all the prayers from my family and friends had reached God's ears: "I just like to think that I am open to the guiding of the Holy Spirit."

As we spoke about the love and grace of God together, the room filled up with witnesses—nurses, the technician, other staff, other patients. Some were cheering, I was hugging the doctor, the doctor was hugging the nurse, and they were all shaking my husband's hand and congratulating the new dad. There we were, sitting in the middle of the ripple effect of this miracle. It seemed as though the entire second floor of the hospital was abuzz.

God is a God of miracles. He is the same God who parted the Red Sea, made manna fall from heaven, and brought the dead back to life. The child who once was lost had been returned to me. The words of Mary in Luke 1 ran over and over in my mind and still do: "My soul magnifies the Lord, and my spirit has rejoiced in God my Savior. . . . For He who is mighty has done great things for me" (vv. 46–47, 49 NKJV).

As I write this, I can still feel the warmth of the buzz from that day. And I can feel my child kicking within me. He is growing bigger by the week, and it won't be long until we meet him face-to-face. I look forward to seeing what good purposes God has laid out for this very special person, but even now I know that my baby is loved, cherished, and known by my heavenly Father. We all are. Every single one of us.

FOURTEEN

An Unexpected Gift

Debbie Morrison

My minivan had broken down again. I was a single mother with a newborn son, living on my own in a new state. Even though I had found a wonderful church, I felt vulnerable, alone, and responsible. And now, standing by the hood of my car, watching Matthew play, I just felt a whole lot worse. How was I going to make the thirty-mile trip to work without my car? How was I going to keep providing for my son when I was on the edge of financial ruin?

God, my best isn't good enough. I can't do it anymore. I need you. I need you to show me that you can take care of my boy and me.

One night shortly after my desperate prayer, Ben, a friend's husband, called me and asked me to meet him down at the car dealership where he worked. He and his wife, Laura, were from my church, and they were both awesome Christians. I didn't really know whether there was any point in going, but my friend said that his wife would watch my son and that I should just trust God and go.

The minute I saw the car I smiled. It was an almost-new Buick Century, and it was beautiful. My friend told me that it was a trade-in from an older couple who had owned it since it was new. It had electric windows, AC, heater, cruise, and a radio that worked, and it was very dependable. It was awesome, and I was sold, but I knew without asking that it was way out of my price range. As I did the math in my head, I tried to see if there was any way I could afford it, but I knew that the thousand-dollar tax check I had received would not get me anywhere close. I lost the smile and started to feel disappointed.

"Thanks," I said. "But I could never afford something like this."

"Well, how much do you have?"

I told him about the tax check. It was all I had, not a dollar more.

"Well," he said, a little smile forming on his face now, "that's a coincidence. A thousand dollars is exactly what this car costs." He handed me a title and sent me on a test drive, and when I came back, the car was mine! I have never cried so hard in my life. God had provided. God had heard my prayer and answered it.

I know that car cost far more than a thousand dollars and that Ben paid the rest of the balance himself. It didn't hit me until later that that was exactly what Christ did for me on the cross. He paid far more than I could have for a gift I could never afford. And in return, he just asks for me to give him all I have.

FIFTEEN

I Give You My Angel

Holly Pugsley

Five weeks after the birth of my second baby, my husband of seven years decided to leave. There I was, with a two-year-old son, a newborn baby girl, and no husband. This was not how I had imagined my life would be. But I was healthy, my two-year-old was healthy, and my not-so-little baby girl who weighed in at ten pounds, eleven ounces when she was born was the kind of baby that everybody looked at with wide eyes and a big smile. They said she looked like a good eater. They said she looked as though she was no trouble. They said she looked healthy. The only thing is, I did not agree with them. I knew something was wrong.

I was referred to a new pediatrician, and my mother went with me to see him. After the doctor finished the examination, he hit me with a question that left me speechless.

"Is there any history of muscle disease in your family?"

All the way home, my mother beside me and my daughter

strapped into her seat behind me, Mom and I said nothing. We were too scared that if we talked, we would start crying and would not be able to stop. There were just so many questions as well. It felt as though my snow globe had been shaken hard again, way before anything had had time to settle.

We were immediately referred to a pediatric neurologist. And so began the long list of visits that my daughter and I made to see people who we hoped could provide us with answers. We saw digestive doctors, genetic doctors, speech therapists, physical therapists, endocrinologists, multiple neurologists . . . you name it; we saw them. For two years we drove to see doctors in hospitals around all of Tennessee, and each one said the same thing. They were not sure what was wrong, but they knew there was a chance she may never walk or even sit up. Some of them told me that I should not even try to teach her to do these things, as her muscles were not developing and we could cause more harm.

And then one day after leaving the endocrinologist, I realized that I could not take any more. I was done—done with all the questions, done with all the uncertainty, done with all the doom and fear and conversations about how my little girl—whom I loved so dearly—was somehow not right. I was done with trying to find an answer, and I was done with putting her through more than any baby should go through. And I was done wasting whatever time I had left running to doctors' offices. There in the car, motionless in the parking lot, I decided to do something different. I decided to have faith, true faith, and let God's will be done no matter what the outcome. I loved my little girl, and for the very first time in my whole life, I felt as though I could trust God completely.

No matter what. So I looked to heaven with tears in my eyes and prayed.

"God," I said, "I give you my angel. Please love her and heal her. Your will be done, as I cannot do this alone."

Within days she began gaining weight. Then she learned to sit. By the time six weeks had passed, my two-year-old girl could stand with assistance. Four weeks later she could stand on her own. By the time she was four, she had caught up developmentally with the other children her age, and by seven she was finally the same size as all the others. And she can do everything—and I mean *everything*—that all the other children her age should be able to do. Today she is an athletic ten-year-old who can ride horses and outrun her brothers.

Of the many doctors who have seen her, none can explain it using medical logic. Instead, they reach for words of faith and call her their "miracle baby." And it's true. It's a God thing! Once I let go of my earthly desire to control things and gave it to God, he showed me how powerful he is. Once I stepped back, he stepped in.

SIXTEEN

Nothing Without God

Anonymous

Not all of us hit rock bottom in our lives. But for those of us who do, the moment that we're down so deep is the moment that the battles for our lives rage like never before. For me, Tuesday, January 12, 2010, was the day my battle was finally fought and won—by God and God alone.

I grew up in a very loving household. My father is a Baptist minister, and my mother is one of the godliest women you could ever meet. I was a true preacher's kid, and by the time I was nineteen, I was a poster child for rebellion against religion.

Discovering alcohol was the worst thing ever to happen to me. But that was not the way I saw it at the time. As a kid fresh out of high school and fresh into trouble, I thought alcohol was my new best friend. I loved to drink. I loved the way it let me feel loose, and it felt good. When I drank, I did not have to think about anything. When I drank, I felt as though I could conquer the world.

At age twenty-one I married my best friend. He was in the marine corps, and I moved around with him to his different duty stations. This was hard for me, and as the good-byes added up, my drinking increased. When he was deployed to Iraq, my drinking reached new levels, and even though lots of people had told me that they thought I might have a drinking problem, I learned how to brush them off.

I became good at telling people what I thought they wanted to hear, and while I was able to sober up from time to time, my life was sinking deeper and deeper. We relocated to Japan, and I started hiding vodka bottles all over the house, throwing away the receipts before I got back from the store, and staying up drinking until the wee hours of the morning, always making it to bed before my husband had to wake up for work. I hated who I had become but not enough to quit.

Before we had left for Japan, I had spent as much time as I could with my grandmother—even though those few occasions were not nearly enough. We had been close for years, and she was getting old. I hated the way she would tell me that once I went to Japan, she and I would probably never see each other again. She kept on wanting to say good-bye, but I told her so many times that it wasn't "good-bye"—it was "see ya later!" Well, she was kind of right. She died while I was in Japan, the same week that my husband went away for a few days. I felt myself plunging to depths I had never experienced before.

With two new bottles of vodka by my side, a box of Kleenex, and an empty house, I sat down to watch the video I had been sent of the memorial service. By the end, I had completely lost it. As I mourned the loss of my grandmother and the loss of who I thought I was, I felt full of self-hatred, guilt, shame, and humiliation. This was my rock bottom. I could not go any lower. I decided there was only one thing I could do: drink myself to death. I stood up from my camping chair and made my way to the kitchen. I would find every last ounce of alcohol I had, search every one of my hiding places that I could find, and drink until I could drink no more.

I was near the kitchen door when a strange feeling stopped me. I felt two hands—one on each shoulder—push me down to my knees. It wasn't that it felt *as if* there were two hands; I physically *felt* them—big, heavy, and warm on my fragile shoulders. My legs could offer no resistance, and I collapsed into a ball. My face to the floor, I began begging and pleading for God to help me. I knew who I had become, and I was more than ashamed of it. I had spit in his face. I had mocked him. I had given my life over to the ways of the world and kicked him to the curb. I knew that I did not—in any way, shape, or form—deserve his love or his help. But I asked for them both.

As I lay there with my face smashed into the carpet, my hands in fists above my head, and my knees curled up by my chin, I asked him to forgive me. I pleaded with him to forgive me. I didn't want to live this lifestyle anymore. I didn't want to go on this way, but I didn't want to die either. I wanted God to take over. I wanted God to bring me home.

Through all my sobbing and all my rambling, I could hear a soft voice in my head saying, *Never will I leave you. Never will I forsake you.* Over and over and over again. Then in an instant I was completely at peace. As though a switch had been flicked, I felt completely sober. Suddenly everything made perfect sense. Even though I had dreaded it so much, moving to Japan was the best thing that could have ever happened to me; it brought me to my knees, desperately in search of God.

I have remained sober to this day. My addiction was taken from me on January 12, 2010, and in return I received something far more precious: the realization that I am absolutely nothing without God.

SEVENTEEN

A Big God and a Tiny Heart

Alan and Candice Hasfjord

I thought I knew fear. I had been in the military, and I had seen enough to know how the body reacts to danger. I knew how fear can mess with you, how it leaves you frozen, sickened, weak. But nothing could have prepared me for the day that I heard the doctor tell my wife and me that Madison, our six-day-old baby girl, was gone.

Nothing I had ever encountered could compare to the power of those words. Nothing had ever made me look so far inward and ask myself how I was supposed to move forward. In the thirty seconds that followed the news, my wife, Candice, and I learned what it means to be truly, completely helpless.

Even today I can still remember what it felt like in that hospital room, and I am still grateful to God for the opportunity to learn what it feels like to have none of your own strength to rely on. And, of course, I'm grateful to God for the miracle that followed.

Her heart had stopped. The monitors drew flat, solid lines across their screens. And then, around two minutes after we were told that Madison was gone, everything changed in the room. Her heart started beating again.

As hard as it is to convey the pain and fear that come with the news that your child has died, it is even harder to explain how getting her back is just as frightening. We weren't sure what to believe. We didn't know what to do. Should we hope that everything was going to be fine, or was this just a brief detour until we would once again be told that she was dead?

The hours that followed were a fog. I saw what was going on around me, but none of it made sense. There were lots of doctors, lots of movement, and lots of tests from lots of machines. I remember talking to several doctors, but for the life of me I couldn't tell you what they said. Candice and I didn't sleep; we didn't eat; we didn't even talk. We simply waited for news.

When it came, however, we both wished it hadn't. We were told that Madison had a very serious heart defect. Those are the exact words, and they are the first ones that I remember hearing in all of that chaos. And they are the words that opened the gates to even more pain and fear than had come before.

The jigsaw of medical information gradually formed, and we began to understand that Madison had been born with an extremely rare and complicated heart condition:

hypoplastic right heart syndrome coupled with a coarctation of the aorta, multiple septal deviations, and a fully roofed coronary sinus. According to the medical team, there was no chance of her surviving what was a seriously deformed heart with a lot of holes and a kinked artery that restricted blood flow. We were told that, although there were proven treatments for hypoplastic left heart syndrome, no baby born with a hypoplastic right heart had survived more than a few weeks. And such an operation could not be carried out in Okinawa. For that, Madison would have to be in a specialist hospital, which meant a fourteen-hour flight back home. And besides, Madison had already suffered so much; when her heart seized in the emergency room, it had triggered a domino effect that began systematically shutting her body down, piece by piece. By the time the medical team had diagnosed the heart condition, she had already suffered liver failure, kidney failure, respiratory failure, and a complete paralysis of her gastrointestinal system.

We were told that the machines were the only things keeping Madison alive, and we should be ready for the charge physician to decide the case. In fact, the hospital case administrator had already called my commander and started the paperwork for emergency leave so we could arrange for her funeral. They had assigned us a case officer to assist us in the process of getting us through Okinawa's customs to return her to our home in the States for burial. They said it was just a matter of time.

Meanwhile, the doctors had transferred her case file to the cardiology team at Rady Children's Hospital in San Diego and arranged for a medevac flight. We were told that these arrangements were merely a formality, as the medical team in Okinawa did not believe they could stabilize her enough to survive the flight. So we just waited—for the customs paperwork to be finalized, for the chaplain to arrange the service coordination at our receiving airport, and for our little girl to do what everyone was telling us she would do. We were waiting for her to die.

For two days we waited. Finally, with the flight, the paperwork, and other arrangements in place, the doctor told us it was now time to leave. Yes, Madison was still alive, but they could not wait any longer. She had to go now even if that meant her not surviving the flight.

Was there a chance she might make it to San Diego? Perhaps, we were told. What kind of chance?

"One or two percent."

And if she stayed here in Okinawa? What chance of survival then?

"Zero."

With that and a few phone calls, we were on our way to the terminal at Kadena Air Base. We were only given a thirty-minute notice, so we left with what we had. It felt good to be moving, to be doing something other than sitting and waiting, and we even laughed at how quickly things were happening. We found dark humor in the fact that during the ride to the air terminal, we both remembered that when we had left the house two days earlier, we had left a pot of spaghetti on the stove, a load of laundry in the washing machine, and the television on.

Fourteen hours later we were in a shuttle bus on our way to Rady Children's Hospital. Madison had survived the flight, and a sliver of hope also landed with us in San Diego. The doctors had been wrong about her not making the flight. Perhaps they might be wrong about the rest of her condition. Maybe she could make it a little farther.

That hope, however, was very short-lived. During her admission to the hospital, the social worker from Rady told us that Madison's acceptance had been granted based upon her condition as related two days earlier. Since then, she had deteriorated to the point where the surgeon would not perform the surgery, as he did not believe she would even survive the anesthesia. The medical team, she told us, would make Madison as comfortable as they could until she passed.

So for the second time in three days, we were guided to a quiet room and made comfortable while we waited for the news that our beloved daughter had died. But, again, God had other plans.

During the early afternoon of December 12, the surgeon called us into his office. He told us very plainly that he didn't know how it happened or why, but Madison's vital signs had stabilized enough that he felt the possible benefits of the surgery outweighed the risks. But he stressed that we should not get our hopes up, for he still believed that there was a very good chance she would never wake up from the surgery. He gave her a 10 to 15 percent chance of making it through. It didn't seem like much, but it was all we had. We signed the release, watched as the medics wheeled her through the operating room doors, and again waited.

The numbness and confusion of those nine hours cannot be described. And even if they could, I am not sure I would want to return to that darkness. But without that long wait there would not have been the sweet rush of limitless hope and joy that came when the waiting room door opened to reveal the surgeon, still in his scrubs, smiling.

In all, over the last four years, Madison has endured four open-heart surgeries, one gastrointestinal surgery, nearly a dozen cardiac catheterizations, and more hospital visits than ten people combined should ever experience. On multiple occasions we have been told that she would not make it, and eventually the words themselves lost all meaning for us.

To this day, no one has been able to tell us how her heart, which never should have begun beating in the first place, suddenly resumed beating after more than two minutes of flat line—not once but twice. No one has ever been able to explain why, after nine weeks in a coma, a baby girl with blood made toxic by liver failure would suddenly begin to breathe past her respirator and open her eyes. No one has ever been able to explain why kidneys that were less than 5 percent functional, lungs that were less than 40 percent functional, and a liver that was less than 10 percent functional would all fully recover with only minor scars.

No one has ever been able to tell us why a little girl who should have died is now, four years later, blessing our family with smiles and laughter and an ageless understanding of who God really is.

No one can tell us why, but to be honest, it really doesn't matter. These are questions we have learned not to ask. These questions do not puzzle us; instead, they point us back to God. We have seen God do so much through Madison; people— yes, even doctors!—have come to faith through witnessing her miraculous recovery, and we have seen ourselves come to a better understanding of who we are and, more important, what he can do through us.

Every medical professional working on Madison's case has told us, at one time or another, that there was no hope. But the Great Physician has taught us that the hope we had was enough to bring her back from death and into glorious life.

EIGHTEEN

Sorrow, Songs, and the Singer

Jordan Skinner

It had taken us a while to accept that we were going to be parents. But by the time she was seventeen weeks' pregnant, my wife and I were finally ready. So what if our situation wasn't ideal? We were going to have a baby, and that was something worth getting excited about.

Just at the point when we were preparing to discover the sex of our child, we were told that we were going to have to say good-bye. Our baby—our son—had died. Carson Lee was stillborn on the morning of February 20.

For the first time in my life, I was not in control. I was helpless and unable to do anything to save my son. From a world once so full of choices—names and nursery colors, first outfits, and cuddly toys—we were suddenly transported to a barren landscape. Our only choices concerned how we wanted to say good-bye. We chose a song by Mark Schultz—"He's My Son"—for the funeral, and as we stood before that tiny coffin, someone from the hospital sang another Mark Schultz song, "Remember Me." Those two songs became our comforters in the days and weeks that followed, and together with support from our families, we were slowly able to overcome the most painful time of our lives.

We found out eight months later that my wife was pregnant again. This second chance, this gift of life, brought with it a mix of happiness and anxiety. But as we passed the seventeen-week milestone, we became cautiously joyful. A week later we were told that we were going to have a precious little girl, and we decided to name her Kyleigh Marie.

In those weeks, every time my wife called me, my heart kicked into panic. The fear was impossible to overcome, and eventually, on January 19, the worst happened. My wife went into premature labor. Our precious Kyleigh was leaving the womb after only nineteen weeks.

The doctors tried to prepare us for what was about to happen: "You will have just a minute or so to spend with her before she passes." One hour and forty-five minutes after she was born, after every family member had been able to hold her and speak loving words to her, Kyleigh's tiny heart gave its last beat. For the second time in a year, our hearts were broken. For the second time in a year, we stood before a tiny coffin and said good-bye. For the second time in a year, we searched for healing within those two songs that had already helped once before.

Four years later, after seven months of bed rest and at full term, my incredible wife gave birth to our miracle baby,

Remington Grace. After six years of pain and grief, our hope was beginning to be restored.

We quickly adjusted to the new rhythms of life, developing new skills that every parent needs. We discovered tag-team eating, formed elaborate rituals for encouraging sleep, and learned that when Remington was screaming in the car, if we tuned the radio to K-LOVE, she got a little happier.

That is how I heard about the Fan Awards—an event for fans to meet some of the people behind the music that K-LOVE plays. With my wife's birthday coming up, it seemed to me like a great way to celebrate. So I crunched some numbers and decided to make it work.

So there we were on the first morning, in line to eat breakfast in the vast dining room of the Delta Ballroom at the Nashville resort where we were staying. There must have been hundreds of tables, and we picked one some ways in. We started to eat, feeling excited about what the event would hold, looking around at all the other music fans. While we were eating, two men asked if they could sit with us. I said yes without thinking anything of it and continued eating.

Two or three minutes must have passed before I looked up and finally noticed who had just joined our table. Half choking on my food, I could only manage to force out my words.

"Mark?" I said.

A big smile came back at me. "Yeah!"

Amazed, I turned to my wife, but she just looked confused. Trying not to speak too loudly, I looked at her and asked, "Do you know who that is?"

"No."

"It's Mark Schultz!"

The tears came to her eyes in an instant. I stood up, held out my hand, and tried to overcome the sudden weakness that was making my knees tremble.

"I don't want to bother you, Mark, but I have to tell you, six years ago, we lost our son, and your song 'He's My Son' changed our lives."

I explained to him that he would never know exactly how much that song meant to us, and that we even had "Remember Me" placed on Carson's headstone. I told him about Kyleigh, too, and watched as his eyes began to tear up as well. While my wife was still sobbing, he walked around the table to hug her, and then—get this!—he asked us if he could have his picture taken with us. He thanked us for sharing our story and told us that our story would stay with him forever. By the time we had finished talking, the other people at the table—all complete strangers—were crying as well.

Out of all the empty tables and all the empty chairs, this man, who had unknowingly played such a powerful role in our lives for the past six years, was led to sit at our table. And in that moment six years of pain, six years of questions, six years of sorrow were changed forever. Our God was there, revealing himself to us that morning. Our God showed us that he cared, that he understood, and that he knew our hearts, our hurts, and our needs even better than we did.

NINETEEN

9/11: Escaping the World Trade Center

Lolita Jackson

I was inside the World Trade Center the first time terrorists tried to destroy it. Like many of my colleagues, I remembered the events of February 26, 1993, as a minor inconvenience. It was an experience that brought old colleagues closer together and served as folklore to share with new employees in the years that followed. While we were frightened at the time, the loss of life was small, and we assumed that none of us would ever experience anything quite like it again in our workplace.

But 9/11 was different. That day saved my life.

I worked for a bank on the seventieth floor of the South Tower. That morning, my entire department was in a conference room in the southwest corner. I was waiting to speak, staring out the window, thinking about how beautiful it looked outside and how—not being a morning person—I wished I were out there. I was looking directly at the North Tower when I saw flames shoot out of the building and papers start fluttering down. My eyes must have grown wide because everyone turned to look at what I had seen. My boss spoke first: "It's time to go."

Almost everyone I was with had been in the building in 1993, and we all remembered how long it had taken us to get out of the buildings that day. So as the fireballs and smoke filled the scene outside the windows, we did not hesitate to leave.

I have believed in God my entire life and have always felt his presence but never more than I did that day. From the moment the first plane hit, I felt as though God himself was holding my hand. Every step of the escape, I sensed him there with me, guiding me, leading me to safety.

Tom, who worked in the office next to mine and was one of my closest colleagues, began walking down the stairs with me. We had not gone far when we were given instructions to get out of the stairwell and take the nearest elevator to the sky lobby on the forty-fourth floor. We exited the fifty-ninth floor stairwell, and Tom said, "I'm going to find an empty office on this floor to go call my wife." I was about to turn to go with him when I heard a voice say, *Don't go!* So I told Tom I would meet him on the forty-fourth floor, and he went off by himself to find an office.

When I exited the elevator on the forty-fourth floor, there were several hundred people gathered around the sky lobby, waiting for instructions. It was the first full week after Labor Day, and many of us had not seen each other in a long time, so the atmosphere was almost festive as we gathered. We just assumed that whatever had happened over on the North Tower was a minor, isolated incident.

Then the second plane hit the South Tower.

Both buildings had been designed to sway in a storm, but this was something else. As the floor shifted beneath me, I thought the building was simply going to fall over, taking every one of us to our deaths. *I'm going to die; I'm going to die*, I said to myself. But then I was suddenly overcome with a sense of peace. I knew that if I died at that moment, I would be okay. I didn't just know I was going to heaven—I could feel it. But the building righted itself, and my thoughts changed. I absolutely knew I was going to get out.

After we were hit by the plane, everyone began streaming toward the same stairwell on the northeast side, away from the side where the plane had struck. Yet I felt God tell me to go to the stairwell closest to where we had been hit. I opened the door and saw that the stairwell was fine—well lit with no debris. I screamed out, "These are clear!" and about fifty people immediately followed me. I led people down the stairwell and tried to encourage them not to think about the trek. When we reached the fifteenth floor, I suggested we call out the floors as though it were New Year's Eve: "Fifteen! . . . Fourteen! . . . Thirteen! . . ."

At 9:26 a.m. I finally exited the complex. The police officers guiding us out were all giving us the same advice: "Don't look up. Don't stop to use your cell phone. Just keep walking." I did what I was told and walked about half a block away, my head down, my eyes focused on my steps. When I did stop and turn around, I froze. People were praying in the streets; the building fires were raging into the sky; chaos was reigning. I stood by myself in the middle of the street and stared. *This is Armageddon*, I thought. What on earth had happened?

"Lolita! Lolita!" Someone was calling my name. I noticed a friend approaching. He consulted for my company but did not work in my building. He had not been inside when the planes hit, so he had a far better idea of what was going on. He told me, "You should go home now. Most of these people can't get home, but you live in Manhattan, and the subways are still running."

It had not occurred to me to leave, but his words made perfect sense to me. We were standing less than one hundred feet from a subway entrance, and I did exactly as my God-sent guardian angel suggested. At about 9:50 a.m. I made my way down into the subway, walked up to the platform, waited a minute for the train that slowly pulled into the station, and sat as it took me home. It was the last train to go through the station that day, and at 9:59 a.m. the first building collapsed. Had my friend not implored me to leave, I would have been running from the dust cloud and quite possibly dodging the debris that shot out at three hundred miles per hour. I know many people who experienced profound physical and emotional trauma as a result of being on the street as the buildings collapsed. They ran for their lives and ducked under cars; they breathed in the all-covering dust; they were the ones who witnessed the horror of people jumping from the North Tower. And I could go on and on.

Tom, my friend who decided to call his wife, entered an elevator approximately three minutes after I did, and he was still in the elevator when it was hit by the airplane. Had I gone with him to make the call, I would have died too.

I suppose that was the realization that changed me the most. Knowing that God had guided me to safety, keeping me out of harm's way throughout the attack, made such a profound impact upon me. Not that I saw it right away, and it took me two years to fully embrace and accept what God had done for me that day. But with that acceptance, he cured me of using work as an idol. That symbol of being on top of the world, working within the Twin Towers, was literally removed. I had no high place to hide anymore. As a result, I began to see that I was finally free to be used by God in ways that he had wanted for me all along. So I changed my career and watched my whole life become transformed.

I never had belonged to a fellowship group but decided to join one to help me through the transition of leaving Wall Street. I became a leader of the group, and through that was nominated for the Redeemer diaconate. I went on my first mission trip and then four more. I became involved in several other ministries and began to get invited to speak at Christian conferences and events all over the country.

God used what could have been solely a tragedy for me and turned it into a soaring triumph. Today I am in a job that serves the city that the attackers tried to destroy, and it is highly unlikely any of this would have happened had I not been ripped away from my complacent life on Wall Street. Where I once was striving only to become a managing director, I now work with a far bigger goal in mind. Every day I live with the knowledge that God saved my life. I know that it was almost taken away, yet in the darkest moment I knew he was right there. God didn't just use 9/11 to change my life. He used it to save it.

TWENTY

Not a Moment Too Soon

Belinda Hogstrom

"Please, Lord, do something!"

I sat on my bed, praying. Nothing unusual about that, but the tears that streamed down my face and the fists that my fingers had formed in my lap told the rest of the story.

"I need a miracle, God. I just can't bear the thought of losing my baby girls!"

I was used to turning to God in my desperation. And in the years that my husband and I had been fostering children, we had both learned to depend on God to see us through all the storms that our chosen vocation brought with it: From the excitement of welcoming new children into our home, to the insecurities associated with our lack of parenting experience. From holding our breath every time a child's parents went to court, to the daily frantic pace of feeding, clothing, educating, and training the ever-changing members of our family. From the grief of losing one child, to the familiar excitement of the new arrival, we had learned that without prayer, we could not cope.

But this was different. And as I sat on the bed and prayed, I knew that I was not praying for the strength or patience or energy to get through the next challenge. I was powerless—completely powerless. My only hope was in God.

A year earlier my husband's job had been transferred, and along with our adopted son, we relocated to another state on the other side of the country. It was at that point that we knew we needed to change things. As foster parents we had cared for twelve different children over the three previous years, but by the time we started unpacking after the move, we were physically and emotionally exhausted. It took us a few days to remember how to breathe and a few days more for our bodies to recall what it felt like to get a full night's sleep.

As my husband started his new job, we began searching for a new home, somewhere permanent, with plenty of trees and land but close enough to the city for the commute. It took several weeks, but eventually we found it: a darling house, complete with painted shutters, a large front porch, and an enormous backyard that would be a perfect place for our young son to run and play as he grew older. The only problem was that it was just on the other side of the county line from where we had been looking. That meant my husband's job and our new church were in one county, and we would be residing in, paying taxes to, using the library of, and being assigned to a school district in another county. No big deal, right? Little did we know how significant that decision would prove to be.

With the job and house taken care of and with life calmer,

now that we were not currently foster parents, we did what pretty much everyone who gets off a roller coaster does after a while—we decided to get back on. We had barely finished unpacking our boxes when we felt compelled to get our foster care license in this new state.

Since every state has a completely independent foster care system, it meant starting all over again—new paperwork, fresh background checks, classes, and home studies. During our licensing interview with the social worker, we explained how—because of our son—we would need to be a little more discerning about what age child we took in.

"We'd like to have a child under the age of two; maybe a girl; perhaps even twins!" I said.

The social worker gave us one of those humorless smiles that said, "Yeah, right!" But even though she lacked a sense of humor, God did not. Not even a full week later, the phone rang, and that same social worker greeted me, saying, "Would you believe that we have just gotten a call from the hospital? They have twin baby girls who are unable to go home with their birth mother. Since you live in the same county where they were born, you would be perfect. Can you take them?"

"Yes!" I said. And after hanging up the phone, I started squealing, laughing, and shaking my head in disbelief. We just happened to be in the right county and just happened to have received our license days before. What clearer evidence was there that God was at work?

The twin girls had been born two months earlier, but because they were so premature (only twenty-eight weeks) and weighed only two pounds each, they had been immediately admitted to the neonatal intensive care unit. The unit's medical staff had efficiently attended to their many needs, coaxing air into their tiny lungs, refusing to accept the failure of their underdeveloped organs, and battling the numerous complications that tend to attack tiny bodies. However, with the combination of the doctors' skills, the babies' strong wills, and the Lord's protective hand, ounce by ounce they gradually grew until they became healthy enough to leave the hospital . . . just days after their new foster parents were ready for them! Of course it was love at first sight, and they were the most precious babies I had ever had the privilege of holding.

Those first few months were pretty much a sleep-deprived fog that I barely remember. But I do remember that as I sat on the couch, feeding one of the babies, rocking the other baby in her bouncy seat with my foot, and reading a story to my two-year-old, I smiled at the thought of God's beautiful sense of humor. And in spite of the physical fatigue, I truly knew without a doubt that God had placed these babies in my care. We were back on that roller coaster once again, and there was no place we would rather be.

One cold night in December my husband and I had gotten home late from a Christmas party. The twins were only a few months old and still quite tiny. I carried them into the house and left them sitting in their car seats on the family room floor while I sat nearby, waiting for them to wake up for their next bottles. I will never know what caused me to glance over at the babies, but when I did, I knew instantly that something was terribly wrong. One of them had skin that was completely pale and lips that had turned the most unnatural color of purplish-blue I had ever seen. She was not breathing.

I snatched her up and was appalled to find her not

reacting to my touch; she was as limp as a rag doll. Almost without conscious thought my hands and mouth automatically kicked into action, desperately trying to breathe life into the eerily still body in my arms. Like every new foster parent, I had attended classes in infant CPR—more than once, in my case. I was so grateful for the training, and I remain so today.

The next few moments seemed like hours before she started coughing; her skin regained its color, and the beautiful pink returned to her lips. Then we both began to cry.

The rest of the night was a blur. A frantic drive to the nearest hospital in record-breaking time. A sleepless night of forms and fluorescent lights and tired eyes as we admitted her to the pediatric floor. A seemingly endless wait for test results while trying not to fear the worst. Then, finally, she was stable enough for me to leave her side.

A few days later, while the first baby was safely recovering in the hospital, we experienced another unexpected dip, courtesy of our life's roller coaster. My husband was working from home while I was out buying diapers. He was keeping an ear out for the baby, who was sleeping in her crib, but when he did not hear her after a while, he went to peek in on her. He saw the same blue lips, pale skin, and lifeless chest that I had seen on her sister the week before. And, like me, he put his own CPR skills into practice that day.

When she was breathing again, he called me, and we made a second urgent trip to the hospital in less than a week. But this time the recovery was not quite so simple and quick. Something was clearly wrong, and the doctors were thoroughly baffled. Fortunately and quickly enough the doctors pinned the breathing problems of both our girls on an infection, and after the antibiotics prescribed did their work, we were able to go home again. Within days, everything returned to normal.

If there is one plain truth that all foster mothers know, it is that when children are placed in their homes, there is a possibility that they will someday leave. But even though we all know this, that fact somehow gets pushed to the backs of our minds. It becomes something to worry about later. Much later.

That distant worry came crashing back into our present shortly after the twins celebrated their first birthday. My husband was hired by another company, and it meant that we would have to relocate to yet another state. It also meant saying good-bye to the twins . . . unless they became free for adoption, something I hoped was about to happen.

Because we were both sure it would not be long before we could adopt the girls, my husband began his new job, moved hundreds of miles away, and planned to come home on the weekends while I remained in our home with the children. But God didn't get my memo. His idea of perfect timing was completely different from mine.

Months went by. There were complications with the birth parents, postponed court hearings, long and lonely weeks as a single parent to an active three-year old and twin one-year-olds, and too-short weekends with my husband. After six months of this madness, I found myself sitting on the edge of my bed, tears running down my cheeks, fists balled up in my lap. Prayer was my only hope.

"Please, Lord, do something! I need your help. My husband is living in a different state. My son needs his father. And

I'm refusing to leave. Oh, Lord, you know that I can't bear the thought of abandoning these girls. How could anyone else possibly love them as much as I do?"

With tears now streaming down my face and my fists now banging against my pillow, I sensed his tender voice whispering to me, *I love them more. Trust me.*

I could almost picture him pointing to my clenched fists and asking me to open them.

Could I do it? Could I let go? Could I really trust God with these precious girls? Reluctantly, but obediently, I opened my fists.

I informed the girls' social worker that we were going to move out of state, contacted a Realtor about selling the house, and began the monumental task of packing our belongings. And all the while I prayed frantic prayers, begging God for a miracle. I knew he could do it. The only question was, did he want to?

Of course, our house sold, and I was unable to procrastinate any longer. I braced myself for the day I knew was approaching quickly, when I would have to say good-bye to my sweet little girls.

I was willing to obey, but that did not mean I had to like it. I was done with roller coasters. I had nothing left.

And then the unexpected happened. The girls' birth parents, who had fought so long and so hard to get their children back, suddenly—and voluntarily—relinquished their parental rights. It meant that the girls were no longer foster children but instead were free for adoption. But time was short—too short, perhaps. Our house was closing in less than thirty days, and unless the paperwork could be done in time, I would still be saying good-bye forever. The case was moved quickly from the foster care department to the adoption department, a new social worker was assigned, and a whole new set of paperwork, references, and home studies was commissioned.

It was almost like sitting back and watching all of the details supernaturally fall into place. And in a breathtaking display of God's timing, on the very same day that the adoption social worker conducted the final interview in our house, the moving van was in our driveway, loading our boxed-up lives.

God had indeed performed a miracle. In his sovereignty he could have chosen to remain silent, to provide another family for the girls, and to gradually heal my wounded heart. But how thankful am I that he did not! Instead, he chose a miraculous intervention, to reach down and open my hands, filling them with treasure beyond measure.

The roller coaster had indeed been heart-wrenching and terrifying, but it was thrilling and exhilarating too. And I would not trade that wild ride for anything.

TWENTY-ONE

Made in Heaven

Michelle Eigemann

I was lying on an ultrasound table, staring at the ceiling in the darkened room, trying not to cry as I listened to the doctors speak about the child growing inside me. One by one they delivered their verdict, laying out the facts the way a mechanic tells you your car is beyond repair.

"He has a broken neck."

"He is bent in half backward, and his head is lying on his butt."

"See that patch there? His bladder has burst at some point."

"There's no amniotic fluid. That means the fetus cannot form properly."

I was trying not to cry, but I didn't think I could hold on much longer.

When the lights came back on, they told me in the strongest terms that I should get an abortion. It would be better for both my son and me, they said. They also told me to have a genetic test to help them understand why this had happened and what kinds of risks there would be in any future pregnancies.

I was a young, unmarried woman at the time. None of this made any sense to me or to the father of my boy growing—or not growing, I guess—inside me. I was lost within this; we both were. And in the midst of feeling overwhelmed, we agreed to do the testing. They sent us home and told us to wait for the results.

That night while I took a bath, I did something I had never done before: I prayed. I had no idea what it meant to know God, but I had heard people talk about it. *Does he hear me as I talk to him?* I didn't know. But I hoped he was listening as I spit out my words in the darkness of my bathroom.

"God, I don't know what you want for my life, and I don't know what you want for the life of this baby inside me. But if this baby is suffering, and if he is too weak to fight, then I want to give him back to you. I will always be his mommy, and I will love and miss him forever, but, please, if he's suffering, let him be yours and not mine."

Immediately I felt peaceful. And at that moment I knew for sure that this baby would be born. Would he be healthy? That I didn't know. But he was going to make it through birth. God had told me so.

Three days later I was back at the hospital, going over the results of the genetic test. According to the ink on the paper, there was nothing genetically wrong with my son. Nothing at all. I smiled, inhaled, and delivered the lines I had been rehearsing for hours.

"I do not want to abort this baby. I want to keep him."

For some reason this took people by surprise. There were discussions, strong words, stark warnings, and clear explanations of the risks I was taking. They told me that even though there was nothing wrong with him genetically, the original scan showed that his body was broken beyond repair. They told me he wouldn't survive the birth. I was taken back to the darkened room, invited to lie down, and administered the cold gel on my stomach before the equipment peered into my womb, the wand moving back and forth across me like an artist painting freely.

I sensed it immediately. The sonographer tensed. The fluid movements of her hand changed in tone. Her breathing quickened.

"What?" I asked. "What is it? What happened?"

"I'll be right back," she said before leaving the room. Before I knew it, she had returned, and the tiny room was full of doctors crowding around the ultrasound screen. I could smell expensive aftershave. Silence followed. Eventually it was broken by three of the sweetest words I have ever heard.

"It's a miracle."

They told me and showed me that my baby's neck was not broken. He had straightened out, and there was no curvature of the spine. I watched as they took me on a tour of my perfect-looking son, who then waved his hand across the screen. I knew it then more than ever—this boy would be born.

It is now seventeen years later, and my boy is in the tenth grade. He has many challenges, but there is no doubt in my mind that he was made for great things, knitted together in his mother's womb by the very hand of God. Life may not be easy, but God reminds our family that we were chosen to walk this broken road, and we believe that God will work all things together for the good of those who love him.

And me? It took a while, but I am a believer now. I am convinced that God pursues us and woos us into relationship with him. He forms us, and he loves us. It's what he does.

TWENTY-TWO

The Dog, the Chicken, and the Bomb

David Newkirk

It was already a night I knew I would never forget. I had watched the seconds count down on the scoreboard, felt my excitement overpower my tiredness, seen heads and shoulders of rival players weighed down by the gravity of defeat, heard cheers and shouts of unbridled joy from friends and family in the stands, and known that, together with my teammates, we had pulled off an incredible victory. University basketball didn't get much better.

The edges of the evening blurred into one another. There were celebrations that flowed from the court to the parking lot, a drive back to my soon-to-be fiancée's house, and then a drive back to my own off-campus house, where my seven roommates wanted a play-by-play of the team's win while they stared at video games. After five hours of soaking in my own sweat, I jumped in the shower and counted down the minutes until I could collapse on my extra-long twin-size bed and surrender to sleep.

Twenty minutes after my head hit the pillow, I was catapulted out of the deepest sleep. I sat upright, suddenly alert, but confused about why. What had happened? Was there someone in my room? Did a siren go off?

Pray for Dan.

What?

Then I heard it again, clear as day, but in my head—

Pray for Dan.

I have been a Christian most of my life and have grown up with stories about God. I know that when you get hauled out of sleep by a powerful command to pray, you don't argue. So I started praying for Dan, my brother.

I need to tell you about Dan before we go further. He's what we all call a blond genius. He is the smartest person I have ever met, but he will get lost crossing the street. He is three and a half years older than me, which means that we grew up playing, hiking, shooting, wrestling, fighting, and breaking down our parents' house. He broke my nose twice. I broke his front four teeth three times. We are very close.

The night I was torn from my sleep, Dan was traveling around the Middle East. September 11 had just rocked our world, and my brother had figured the airfare might never be cheaper, so he headed out to see the sights of Jordan, Syria, Egypt, Turkey, and Israel. He was sure this was a stroke of genius while others thought it was more of a blond decision.

I hadn't heard from Dan in about a week. At six foot three and 220 pounds, he could take care of himself, but when I heard a voice in my head telling me to pray for him, I knew I must.

The house was silent as my quiet prayers eased into the darkness. For more than an hour I asked God to protect my brother, to send angels and push back the danger, to keep him safe from harm. And then, almost as suddenly as the adrenaline had spiked me awake, I felt God's peace rest on me, and I fell back asleep.

The next morning I called my parents.

"Have you heard from Dan?" my mother asked right away, firing off the same question I had intended to ask. Now I was worried.

"No, Mom. I haven't heard from him, but last night I woke up and knew I had to pray for him."

"Me too! I was awakened and knew I needed to pray for Dan. And I just talked to your older sister, and she was abruptly woken to pray for him also."

None of us knew anything more than this, and since Dan was not answering his phone, we did what we could; we waited a while longer, prayed, and trusted that the same God who had shaken us all awake was by Dan's side in whatever he was going through.

Two or three hours after I had spoken with my mom, an e-mail came through. When Dan's name flashed up on my screen, everything else stopped. I read his words as though they were the only words in the world:

TO: David Newkirk; Mom & Dad; Kari Newkirk
SUBJECT: Last night . . .

Last night I was in Israel, and I was tired. I'm running out of money, so I decided to sleep in a public park. I found an empty picnic bench near a bus stop and rolled out that big old mummy sleeping bag that David and I used to fight over. I was exhausted. It must have been almost morning—even though it felt like the middle of the night—when one of the scariest experiences of my life occurred. I was completely zipped up in the bag, with just my face showing, when I was jerked awake by the angry snarling and barking of a dog. I was trying to get out of this death trap of a bag, but I couldn't find the zipper! And this crazy dog was snarling and barking just by the bench, and all I could think of was that I was going to be eaten by a rabid dog! Finally, covered in sweat, I grasped the zipper, yanked it down, and jumped out of the bag and onto the ground, ready to defend myself. The dog was madder than anything, but once I got away from the bench I could see what was bothering him—it was not me but a chicken that was hiding under the bench. Calming down—and talking myself out of taking care of both of them permanently—I tried to shoo them away. They completely ignored me and carried on their battle of the bench. Frustrated and cold, I decided to give it up. I picked up my stuff and moved to a picnic table about 100 yards farther into the park.

I woke up with the sun on my face and started packing. Still tired, I sat and made myself some cold instant coffee and watched the sun climb up into the sky. Just as I was figuring out where I had tossed my map in all the chaos of the night before, I was thrown to the ground by an explosion.

I looked over toward the street and saw a bus burning.

What?! In front of it, instead of the bench where I had settled the previous night, was a mess of tangled metal and concrete. The bench itself—what was left of it—had been blown right across the park. If it hadn't been for that stinking dog and that chicken . . .

Three people torn from sleep to pray for a guy bundled up in a winter sleeping bag while a dog chased a chicken around a park bench that was hours away from being ripped apart by a bomb. How could this crazy, wild story of protection and care be anything other than a God thing?

TWENTY-THREE

An Angel in a Nurse's Uniform

Krystina Potter

I do not remember the first time it happened, but I know the first memory I have of it. I was seven, playing basketball in the gym. Without warning, everything in my vision turned to a hazy yellow, and my heart felt as though it was going to pound right out of my chest. I looked down and could see my shirt trembling with the force of my heart. I became dizzy, and sweat fell from my forehead. While it did not seem real at first, when I realized that the pounding was not going to stop, I began to panic. I called my coach over and was immediately sent to the nurse's office. Only after she splashed cold water on my face did the pounding stop. But the real trauma had only just begun.

A year later I was diagnosed with Wolff-Parkinson-White (WPW) syndrome. Most kids at that age are used to racing around, getting their heart rates up as they play. But my heart would do the racing all on its own. I could be sitting around, still as a leaf, when I would feel my chest pounding. Every day I feared a WPW attack, and I never knew when one might come on. Death was never far from my thoughts, and I felt as though I were in some way defective.

By the time I was twelve, I had been to see so many doctors and waited in so many sterilized rooms that I was used to the sounds that fill the hospital air: the bleeps of machines, the soft murmur of busyness, the cries of discomfort. I was admitted for a catheter ablation procedure. It sounds harmless enough, but the truth is that they stick electrodes in your chest and try to kill off the bits of your heart that are malfunctioning. If it sounds brutal, I guess that's because it is. To make things worse, I was one of only a handful of children who were having this procedure done at this point; the staff were at the start of a steep learning curve.

The moment I first woke up from the anesthesia, I gasped for air. A fire went off in my chest, and I felt such pressure in there that it scared me. I could see a tube coming out from my chest, and it was full of blood. I traced its path with my eyes and saw that it was connected to a machine that made gurgling noises. My surgery had not gone well. Not at all, in fact. The anesthesiologist had mistakenly stuck a needle too far down into the artery that runs under my collarbone, resulting in a collapsed lung.

I was placed in an adult intensive care unit so I could be monitored appropriately. I was twelve years old, surrounded by adults with heart conditions. Some had had heart attacks; others were in comas. My fear increased.

That first night, I lay there, alone. I was in horrible pain from the chest tube, and the noises of the machine to my side were incessant and terrifying. Each breath I inhaled was difficult, and I was scared of the next one. I was very anxious and wanted to go home. I remember wondering what I had done to deserve this. I had never felt so alone in all my life.

I had been listening to the sounds of the rooms around mine, trying to acclimate myself, trying to find something I could hold on to, when a new sound rang out. The steady *beep, beep, beep* of the machine in the room next door changed and became a single, solid note, held without breath. I heard someone yelling, "Code blue! Code blue!" and within seconds the speakers in the ceilings repeated the words. I listened as people came thundering into the room next to mine. I listened for the man in the bed, but he made no sound. The nurses spoke in clipped, serious tones. I listened as they stopped, and I knew he had died. I wondered if anyone would come take him away.

I was terrified.

Shortly after that a figure appeared in the doorway. It was a nurse I had not seen. She told me her name was Karen, and as she sat next to me, she reached out and held me. She had light skin with lots of freckles. I will never forget her soft, curly red hair; her thick glasses; and her soothing, calming voice as she read to me. She spent the rest of the evening comforting me, and I had never before experienced so much peace. Eventually I slept.

I woke up the next morning, and she was gone. When my dad came in, I told him about Karen and how she had been so kind and helpful. Like any parent would do, he went to the nurses' station to thank her, but when he described her as I had—the hair, the freckles, the glasses, and the kind way in which she stayed with me all night—he received nothing but blank stares and shaking heads.

No nurse by that name or description had ever been employed there. Karen, they said, did not exist.

Today I am thirty-three years old, and I know that I have been forever changed by this experience. Since that first procedure, I have undergone two more. There have been no more collapsed lungs, but the memory of Karen has helped me through nonetheless. I have been told that my condition is rare and that things may get worse as I get older. However, when I think of all this, Karen's face comes into my mind, clear as that day in 1992, and I still feel comfort. I know my heavenly Father has me in his hands. With him, I am never alone.

TWENTY-FOUR

Thanking God for Unanswered Prayers

Ray and Betty Whipps

Awakened by a hail of bullets that tore through the barn like fireworks on a Fourth of July night sky, Ray knew there was only one way out. "Comrade!" he shouted in his halting German. "I surrender!"

Sergeant Ray Whipps had been through plenty of terror in this war. He had staggered up the beaches in Normandy, taken his chances in the Battle of Hürtgen Forest, and watched many men die in foxholes and on medics' stretchers. Was this now the time for him to join the fallen? If it was, then at least he might get an answer to the constant question that had plagued him these last three years: Why had so many of his prayers gone unanswered? Why had his requests of God—to serve his country as a pilot, to offer his life alongside the men he had trained with—been greeted with not just silence but a clear and final *no*?

In the courtyard outside the barn, it was dark. Ray was stripped of his gear and made to wait as the German soldiers continued searching the village for others. He knew they would find none, for he had been alone when he entered the village the previous night. Separated from his platoon, exhausted, and wrung out from so many months fighting for survival, Ray had given in to the exhaustion that gripped his body and soul and had slept. He had not prayed for it all to be over, but perhaps this was the ending that God had been leading him to all along. It made no sense, but then so little did in this war.

Ray had come a long way from the cornfields that quilted the landscape of Columbus, Ohio. As a child he longed to fly, and his hopes and prayers were almost answered when he was admitted into the Navy Air Corps. But almost wasn't quite enough, and though his test scores were not bad, they prevented him from making it through to the final phase of training. And though he had sixty hours of flying time, he could not get his wings. There was no spot in a plane for Ray Whipps.

Despite this setback, when the draft letter came, he was ready to serve as an army infantryman. Basic training brought Ray and his platoon together, strengthening the bonds of trust and friendship that would be so vital to their success—and survival—once finally deployed. But when the regiment was about to be shipped, Ray was told that he would not be joining them. He was to stay back in Florida, training the next batch of recruits before shipping out with them. Again Ray was left facing a door that had closed unexpectedly, and again he was left asking, "Why?" And when news of his former platoon's fate reached him—how they had taken part in the Utah Beach operation and how three thousand Allied troops had lost their lives in the shallow waters and bloodstained sands on June 6, 1944—Ray's questions became only louder.

Now the skies above were silent. The German soldiers who had captured him looked tired, defeated—almost. Ray knew that even though they were retreating from the Allied forces, when he was ordered to march, he could do nothing but comply.

As he walked in the darkness, Ray's mind played back the events of the war so far. He recalled his injuries that had twice taken him off the front lines. First it was his hands, lacerated by shrapnel and flying debris as he dodged the bombs that fell on the ruins of Saint-Lô. He had felt so different then, and the injury had left him both scared and grateful—scared that the war had the power to make any second his last, yet grateful he had been kept from harm so far. But still the prayers, still the question, "Why?"

After his hands had recovered enough to allow him to hold and fire a rifle again, Ray was sent back to join his platoon, now deployed in Hürtgen Forest, a fifty-square-mile killing zone of steep hillsides, deep ravines, and enemy assaults. More than one hundred thousand Allied troops had gone into the woods, and their lifeless bodies were being pulled out by the thousands. And when a mortar exploded at his side, Ray's leg became a ball of white-hot pain, shredded flesh and muscle. It was all he could do to force himself to his feet and limp back out, past scores of dead bodies.

The injuries that Ray had sustained, as well as the nameless horrors he had witnessed, gave even more volume to his questions. Why was God doing this? Why, when all those prayers to be a pilot had gone unanswered, was his life's path weaving so close to death? Was he being played with, like a wounded mouse at the claws of a cat?

While recovering in Cherbourg, France, in a military hospital made of tents, Ray had searched his Bible for answers. Psalm 37 was a favorite, and the instructions not to fret, to commit and trust God, to rest and wait for Jehovah, all spoke deep into his soul. He sang, too, filling the air around his cot with songs of faith and hope, such as "Jesus Loves Me."

And that was when it happened. That was when the first glimmer of an answer revealed itself to him—and her name was Betty Jean Carter. She was a nurse, but to Ray she was more like an angel with hazel eyes. As she dressed his wounds, they talked. And as they talked, a deep friendship grew. When he and Betty spoke—especially about the faith in God they both shared—Ray felt his questions easing, not because she was a distraction but because Betty had been asking the same questions all along.

Like Ray, Betty had wanted to serve her country, wearing a navy uniform. She had applied, only to be told that her slight overbite would surely make her prone to seasickness.

Of course it did no such thing, and while crossing over the Atlantic, Betty was one of the few nurses who didn't suffer. But rules were rules, and Betty's prayers to serve in the navy were blocked. As she and Ray spoke, they discovered that just two weeks separated Ray's exit from the Navy Corps from Betty's bizarre rejection.

More plans and prayers followed for Betty as she again set her heart on a specific role: serving in a field hospital close to the front lines. Again, the answer was no, and to her surprise she found herself far from the battles and in Cherbourg. With Ray.

Thirty days after Ray arrived in Betty's care, his new orders were delivered. He was being transferred to a recovery facility in England, where he would rehabilitate his leg and prepare to join a combat platoon. The night before he left, he called Betty to his bedside and held out a ring that he had carried on his dog tags.

"Betty," said Ray, "when this war is over and we go back home, will you marry me?"

"Of course, Ray. Of course I will."

For five days Ray marched, each step taking him farther away from Betty and farther away from the one thing that made sense out of all the false starts and closed doors. At some point Ray found out where they were heading—Munich—and by the time he arrived and was thrown into a cell with two other GIs, Ray's fears were confirmed—they were to be shot in the morning.

Others might have given up on prayer by this point, but not Ray. Falling to his knees, Ray was still on the floor that night when he and the other soldiers were thrust out of their cell. An air raid siren had sent the place into a panic, and once the American bombs finished pounding the city, Ray and the other prisoners were sectioned off and forced to march north to Stalag VII-A.

With Ray already weak and exhausted, the short march all but destroyed him. His feet were in agony, and his cracked lips cried silently for water. If not for the kindness and bravery of a German soldier, who disobeyed the orders of an SS officer, Ray would have been executed at the side of the road. Was this a glimmer of hope or just another twist in the slow descent toward death? Why was God letting this happen? Was Betty his God-ordained future or just a brief encounter before the final act?

But the worst was still to come. As Ray stumbled into the infamous prison camp, he entered a nightmare world of disease, malnutrition, and despair. Ray's finger had been wounded in the prison raid and was growing infected, and with no access to medication or doctors, a fellow prisoner boiled a pot of water three times a day and forced Ray to submerge his wounded finger. The blistering hot pain dropped him to the floor, but thankfully his friend would not give up. Within a week the infection was gone, but Ray was left clinging to the very last shred of life. Was this how it was going to end?

It was not.

On May 1, 1945, one month after he was captured, Allied forces liberated Stalag VII-A and the eight thousand Allied troops being held there. Finally Ray's questioning could ease, and he was free to return home in search of the answer he knew to be right.

Five months later Betty Jean Carter and Ray Whipps were married in a Baptist minister's home in New Orleans, Louisiana. Sixty-seven years later, with seven children, eighteen grandchildren, and twelve great-grandchildren, their search for God in the midst of tragedy and suffering is still bearing fruit. And though so many brave lives were lost in the midst of it, Ray and Betty's is a story of God's faithfulness and care transcending our limited understanding.

An injury at just the right time, a deployment to just the right place, and a German officer willing to save an American soldier's life. But it is clear that God also used the unanswered prayers, the silence, and closed doors to bring about his will. The understandable doubts, questions, and disappointments that both Ray and Betty experienced did nothing to weaken their faith or God's power to act. And in each twist and turn, we can see a wink from the divine, the always present God, ever working behind the scenes, still moving in mysterious ways.

TWENTY-FIVE

The Miracle of the Son

Elizabeth Cavanaugh

October 13, 1917. The people gathered in thousands, forming a crowd as large as a forest. They had come to the field outside the little Portuguese village of Fatima because three young shepherd children had told them that, at noon, there would be a miracle. Few were disappointed. As one of the many journalists who witnessed the event wrote, "The silver sun, enveloped in the same gauzy grey light, was seen to whirl and turn in the circle of broken clouds. . . . The light turned a beautiful blue, as if it had come through the stained-glass windows of a cathedral, and spread itself over the people who knelt with outstretched hands . . . people wept and prayed with uncovered heads, in the presence of a miracle they had awaited. The seconds seemed like hours, so vivid were they."*

---

* John J. Pasquini, *The Existence of God: Convincing and Converging Arguments* (Lanham, MD: University Press of America, 2010), 49; *Wikipedia*, s.v. "Miracle of the Sun," http://en.wikipedia.org/wiki/Miracle_of_the_Sun.

That day became known as the Miracle of the Sun, and ninety-three years later, the date developed a special meaning for me and my family. I was pregnant at the time, and the previous months had not been easy. From time to time I would have a sensation within me that I could only describe as a seizure. It was almost violent, like a very rough shaking, and would last about a minute. It was not at all like a normal baby kick or movement that I was used to from my previous pregnancies. It happened at least half a dozen times, and on each occasion I was hooked up to monitors and told to lie still and wait. After an hour or so the doctors would come in and tell me that everything was just fine with my baby and then send me home. I knew they were wrong.

When they discovered that I had severe preeclampsia, they induced me. My due date was not for another five weeks, but they felt it was worth the risk. And so Mary Grace was born on October 13, 2010, right on the anniversary of the Miracle of the Sun. She was so tiny, at just over four pounds, and was sent to the NNICU for observation. Once she was in the unit, her seizures—which I had been so convinced of while she was inside me—started up again. The terrible fits were almost impossible for the staff to control. Medication did not work, and with every seizure she stopped breathing, risking brain damage. Once they did a CT scan, they discovered that my little Mary Grace did have a problem, and it was a bad one—a blood clot in her brain.

An MRI confirmed the clot. Worse was the news that it was getting bigger. The doctors told my husband and me that Mary Grace must have had a stroke in the womb, and the result of the clot was that the cerebral sinuses were prevented from forming. These venous sinuses are vital, draining blood away from the head. Our little girl was missing something that was essential for life, and the doctor was clear on how serious the situation was. Mary Grace no longer had pupil dilation or a gag reflex, both of which are instinctual; even people in a coma have these reflexes. And added to the problems were the staph infection and pneumonia caused by being on the ventilator so long. Eventually we were told that there was nothing that could be done for her. The only decision for us to make was when to turn the machines off and say good-bye to our beautiful baby girl.

But we felt there was one other thing we could do for Mary Grace before we said good-bye. We asked the priest to visit and anoint her and pray for peace, just as it says we should do in James 5:14–15. As he arrived and waited in the doorway, my husband turned to him, smiled, and said, "You know we are expecting a miracle. No pressure!"

It was such a strange day. I know it seems hard to understand, but we felt really good that day. We had done all we could do. Now it was up to God and God alone. Mary Grace was in his hands now, not ours. We went home that night to be with our other children. We prayed and tried to rest for what was to come. It was really a time of anticipation; we knew that whatever happened would be God's plan, but, of course, we were hoping and expecting that the miracle that God would provide would be one in which Mary Grace stayed with us. That was our hearts' desire, and there was a sense of being empowered as we and others from the church prayed.

There had been so little that we had been allowed to do

for Mary Grace since she was born; even touching her was limited. We believe that there is grace in the sacraments, an outpouring of God's love for us that is there for us when we need it. That night we felt at peace because we had done all that we could so that our daughter would know Christ and his church during that time.

The next day I woke up feeling excited. I couldn't wait for what came next. This was the day we would remember for the rest of our lives. As we drove to the hospital, we were quiet, as we had been so many other times while visiting Mary Grace. The drives to the hospital—as well as our time by Mary Grace's incubator—had been very quiet. During times of great pain, there really are no words to adequately express how you feel. It almost seems that if you were to open your mouth to speak, an avalanche of pain would consume you. So, as we drove in, parked the car, and walked across the lot, we held hands and hugged.

Approaching the doorway to the NNICU, I saw one of the nurses standing outside. She looked up as we approached, tears covering her face. She was waiting for us, and I thought it was odd that they would tell us in such a public place that our little girl had died. Shouldn't they be taking us into a quiet room, offering us a seat and a long explanation of how it all happened?

The nurse did not say anything; she just opened the door and urged us through. Maybe someone else was going to tell us. Maybe they wanted us to see for ourselves that she had died. But as we walked into the unit, passing the other babies laid out beneath ultraviolet lights in their cribs that looked like space capsules, we saw her. My girl, my baby girl, was alive. Her eyes were open, her body was wriggling, and she looked like a brand-new baby. She was alive!

Through the tears and the prayers and the hugs, we heard the doctors tell us that we should not expect too much from Mary Grace. They told us that the best we could hope for was cerebral palsy, but I didn't care! She was alive!

A couple of days later they repeated the MRI, searching for the clot. But it wasn't there. It had vanished completely. They searched for a sign of brain damage, but again, they could find nothing but a healthy, normal-looking brain.

Two years later Mary Grace is a typical, energetic girl. She gets into everything and is totally spoiled by her older sister and five brothers. The doctor still cannot explain it, but we know the truth. We know that our girl, who was born on the day that celebrates the Miracle of the Sun, was blessed with a miracle that came straight from the Son himself.

TWENTY-SIX

Midnight Stranger

Kathleen Kohler

"You can't keep going like this, Ben. You're burning the candle at both ends. Your body is not a machine." Ben was seventeen, and I—like all mothers trying to change their teenager's lifestyle with a ten-second lecture—knew what was coming next.

"Oh, Mom, I'm fine," he said, his hand waving through the air, brushing aside my concern. "You worry too much," he added as he headed out the front door for work. I watched him climb into his pickup and barrel down the driveway in a cloud of dust and out onto the rural road that would take him the twenty-two miles into town. Clearly, it was going to take more than a ten-second lecture to make him see sense. So I did what I had done so many times before and offered up the quickest of prayers in the hope that God himself would keep my little boy safe.

My reactions were no different from other mothers', and

Ben's attitude was no different from his friends'. They all think they're invincible at that age, and Ben had the workload to prove it. Besides school, he had started a landscape business two years earlier that kept him busy on weekday afternoons, and when he bought his truck, he took on a weekend job at the movie theater to help pay for the insurance.

At twelve thirty that night I was still awake, listening for the familiar sound of Ben's truck pulling up to the house. My husband, Loren, had been concerned, but he had to get some sleep because he had work the next day, so he lay snoring gently beside me. Yet by now, Ben was thirty minutes late. There was no way I was sleeping.

At one thirty, the noise of someone banging on the front door pulled me bolt upright in bed. I sped out of the bedroom, wondering whether Ben had forgotten his key and why on earth he was so late, when—passing through the living room—I saw an unfamiliar shape waiting on the porch. It was not Ben.

Anyone who has ever opened the door in the middle of the night to a uniformed police officer knows the speed with which the chill spreads through your body. My throat tightened instantly, my heart started pounding, and my hands shook intensely as I grasped the knob to unlock and open the door.

The officer asked if I was Ben's mother.

"Yes, I'm his mother," I heard myself say as if watching a movie clip in slow motion. "Is he okay?"

"Your son's alive, but he's been in an accident," said the patrolman. He didn't know Ben's condition, but he assured me that Ben had already arrived at the hospital.

"From the looks of the tire tracks, he made no attempt to stop," the officer said.

Through tears I managed to choke out, "I'm sure he fell asleep."

"Well, he's one lucky boy. If he'd gone off the road fifty feet in either direction, he'd be dead for sure."

I knew the location that the officer described. Like so many roads in Washington State, the one that ran from our house to Granite Falls cut through thick forest. Ben had crashed right into a section where the solid wall of 150-foot fir trees that edged both sides of the highway gave way to a short patch of swampland. Was Ben a lucky boy? Luck had nothing to do with it.

It was only later that we learned what had really happened. As I had guessed, Ben had been exhausted from the long hours he was working, and as he drove the long road home, sleep had taken over. His truck careened off the dark road, down the steep gravel bank, and into the swamp. Several pieces of glass from the windshield had embedded themselves in his skull, and he had a four-inch gash on the right side of his head. When he saw the headlights of a car speed by— without pausing—on the road above, he knew that his only chance of getting help was if he made it out of the car by himself and onto the road.

The truck lay on the passenger's side in the swamp. The impact had jammed the door shut, but by lying across the bench seat and kicking hard at the sunroof, Ben was able to break free. He crawled from the vehicle, splashed into the water-filled swamp grass and tall strands of cattails, and— with blood running down his face and soaking into his jacket—clawed his way up the bank and onto the highway.

Ben had driven the road countless times and knew that

the closest help was the unmanned fire station five miles away. He set off, stumbling yet numb from the pain of the impact, and hoped he would reach the station in time.

After fifteen minutes Ben heard the sound of a car approaching from behind. He turned and saw headlights, which eventually came to a stop on the gravel in front of him. Ben told the driver what had happened, and before going for help, he assessed Ben's injuries. He helped Ben into his car and drove him to the volunteer firehouse, where he sounded the alarm. And then, as quickly as he had arrived, the stranger left Ben seated on the ground outside the building and drove away.

Within twenty minutes firefighters arrived at the station, loaded Ben into the aid car, and worked to stop the bleeding. They called ahead to the nearest town, where paramedics waited for them to arrive and then rushed Ben to the closest hospital thirty minutes away, where he could receive the blood transfusion he urgently needed.

By the time Loren and I walked through the doors of the hospital, into the bare lighting that bounced off the walls, Ben was stretched out on a gurney in the emergency room. From behind the mess of tubes, needles, IVs, doctors, and nurses, he smiled and said, "I'm okay, Mom."

Hearing his voice and seeing him alive unlocked great waves of tears from within me. In that moment my shoulders relaxed, and the tension subsided.

"Someone was watching out for him," the ER doctor said. "Another fifteen minutes and he would've bled to death."

Hours later, once the gash on Ben's head had been stitched up, we were allowed to take him home. For several days we tried to find the man who had driven Ben to the fire station so we could thank him. We asked around the area if anyone knew who had picked our boy up that night, but strangely, in a community of fewer than three hundred people, no one could identify the man.

We never did discover his identity. Whether he was simply an anonymous stranger or a guardian sent from heaven remains a mystery. All we do know for sure is that both through the location of the accident and the timely arrival of the stranger on the scene, Ben encountered a miraculous rescue that night. And a powerful reminder that Mom always knows best!

TWENTY-SEVEN

Out of the Blue

Anonymous

I opened the door to the bedroom, and that's when I saw him—my husband. Lying on the bed. I thought he was sound asleep, but as I called to him, he didn't stir. On the bedside table I saw the empty bottle of pills. And then the note. It was to our children. To them my husband had simply written, "Sorry, but this is no way to live."

For years he had battled depression, and as seasons came and went, we both noticed how, when the winter weather set in, he oftentimes started to feel a little better. But as the days got longer and the sun rose higher in the sky, his depression would burn with a fiercer flame within him.

Standing by his still-breathing body, I looked outside the window. I saw nothing but blue skies and a bright shining sun. For most people weather like this is cause to celebrate life. For my husband, it led him to embrace death. I shook him, desperately trying to wake him, but it was no use. He was unconscious. In a daze, still clutching the empty pill bottle and the note, I wandered out to where my son was chopping wood in the forest. He took one look at me and took charge of the situation as he ran to the house, yelling for someone to call 911. He stayed with his dad until the medics arrived. Time was running out.

This story is not so much about the miracle of my husband's survival. It is not about the fact that I heard God's still, small voice urging me to go see if he wanted some breakfast rather than just leave him alone. It is not about the fact that the medics arrived in time to give him oxygen and whisk him away to the helicopter, which delivered him to the hospital. My story is about the miraculous way in which God provided for us as we both tried to recover.

"God will provide."

I cannot tell you how many times I have heard those words. Preachers, singers, friends, and even random strangers—I have heard them all say it. Perhaps it is because I have Parkinson's disease that I have found those words difficult to understand. I don't know for sure, but I do think that it was not until my husband's suicide attempt and the ensuing months of treatment and rebuilding of relationships that I finally understood what it is to really know that God provides.

As the ambulance disappeared down the road, we gathered our things together and set off for the next ferry that would take us to town. We found our way to the hospital waiting area, where, amid many hugs and tears, we waited for my husband to wake up. As the time passed by slowly, questions kept running through my mind. Why would anyone do this to his family? How was he going to feel when he woke up and found he had failed in his attempt? Would he be grateful? Disappointed? Embarrassed? Shamed? Angry?

As the hours passed, more and more family and friends gathered in the hallway outside the recovery room. When he finally woke up, he tearfully apologized to each person there. He was well loved during those next few hours.

The next five weeks would find me riding the ferry and visiting the hospital daily. My husband spent his time receiving shock treatments and counseling and experimenting with what would be the best antidepressant to use. The doctors would not release him until they felt he would be safe back home—that he would not hurt himself or anyone else. But all that takes time. Time to break through old habits and mind-sets and rebuild relationships damaged by the depression.

While we both understood the importance of keeping him hospitalized, with every week that passed, we knew the stack of medical bills was growing taller. Insurance would cover much of it, but not all. With bills as big as these, even the small percentage that we would have to pay was enough to leave me feeling overwhelmed. With me being unemployed, battling a serious illness myself, what hope did we have of making it out?

I shared my concerns with my best friend from high school. How was I going to pay for this? How were we going to get through it without going under? She asked if she could share my dilemma with other close friends from high school. I agreed. I needed all the prayers and support I could get. And, of course, she wanted me to remember one simple thing: God would provide.

A few days after we met, she called back. She told me that it was all taken care of; an old friend of ours who had been incredibly successful in business had agreed to cover all our medical expenses. She told me that he wanted to give something back to the people who had been important to him over the course of his life and that a check was in the mail.

I was blown away. I had never known such kindness. And when the check arrived, it was enough to cover all our medical expenses and help us through a further year and a half of unemployment. If ever I have doubted in my life about God's love and provision, I could no longer deny it one bit. God had provided—and how!

This generosity changed our lives in so many ways and not just the obvious ones, like releasing the burden of worry and allowing me to care full-time for my husband as he worked toward recovery. It changed the way I react to others when they are in need as well. For instance, last week I heard of a friend who was having a hard time with his business, and I felt compelled by the Lord to send him a check to get him through this time, plus some extra. The joy and relief he expressed over my small gift were all I needed. It blessed my day as well. I now understand the old saying, "It is more blessed to give than to receive."

I have also learned not to be afraid or ashamed to share the difficult times, to share the struggles, to share the weaknesses in life. If I had kept those struggles to myself, I would have missed out on a couple of incredible blessings. I would not have learned firsthand that God really does provide. I would not have learned the truth of the words of James 4:2: "You do not have because you do not ask" (NKJV).

TWENTY-EIGHT

Saved. Saved. Saved!

Steve Kaliszewski

My earliest memories are of my life being a mess. By the time I was ten, I had attempted suicide and been sexually abused by an older boy in the neighborhood. Every day brought with it a constant stream of ridicule and verbal abuse from kids in school, and every day began and ended with the incredible tension that seemed to fill every room of my home. I simply did not want to live.

I learned some tricks to help me cope, but the truth was they only made things worse. I would smile and laugh to cover up the intense effort it took to hold myself together, but my tricks only reminded me how unhappy I was. I spent as much time as I could away from home, but that reminded me how little I belonged. I listened as I was praised by my relatives for being successful, for being their favorite, and I tried to live up to their expectations, but doing so reminded me how worthless I felt inside.

My parents divorced shortly after I finished high school. With their separation came a change within me too. I started blaming other people for my problems and refused to take responsibility for my own actions. In college I was part of the cool fraternity, and for the first time in my life, I was noticed and liked. For the first time ever, I was popular. I took in all I could of the things that were offered: parties, alcohol, drugs, women, attention, and status. I hoped they would ease my pain, but they only took me right back to the beginning. All that excess only reminded me of how empty I felt.

I thought I could escape all of that by joining the marines, and in a way I did. But things didn't work out quite the way I thought they would. I was part of the infantry community and deployed to Iraq. Where we were operating, we were not fighting a few men but the whole village. And our enemies made what we called *triple stackers*—IEDs comprised of three artillery shells placed on top of each other, buried in the ground, and detonated at the precise moment an American convoy passed. Those artillery shells are powerful—imagine a bullet about twenty-four inches long, nine inches wide, and weighing about forty pounds. Put three of those in a hole and detonate. Even a Humvee doesn't stand a chance.

On this one specific mission we had found a stack of enemy weapons and needed to detonate them. My team was setting up C4 explosives around the cache while I was stopping local traffic from getting too close. I had to cross a road with my point man to set the perimeter when my radio scratched out its message: "five minutes to controlled det." I had plenty of time to get away before the weapons were to be destroyed in a huge explosion, but about ten seconds after the message,

I heard the most deafening boom of my life. Turned out there was a wire running alongside the road, connected to another bomb that had been well hidden. While I was approaching it, an Iraqi local set off an IED on me. My team watched as the blast engulfed the whole of the two-lane road, and without even a doubt in his mind, our radio operator got ready to call in to our command and tell them that I was KIA.

But I wasn't. Instead, like my point man, I was alive although I had no idea what had happened. I found myself twenty feet away from the road, on my knees, shaking uncontrollably. I asked my point man to do a blood sweep, running his hands under my body armor, front and back. Nothing. Not even a scratch. It made no sense; being that close to such a large blast, I should have been pink mist. All of me—except maybe my flak jacket, my Kevlar helmet, and my M4 rifle— should have been destroyed. I should have died in an instant, but I was alive.

Three months later I was struggling again. This time it was the transition back into civilian life that I was dealing with, and it remains the hardest thing I have ever encountered. I would sit on my couch and cry for hours, trying to figure out why I was still alive while so many brothers were not. The plan and vision I had for life after the marines seemed good enough in theory, but nothing was working out for me.

I had waited tables while I was in college, so I thought I might as well do that again. But it was nothing like the way I remembered it. Just a few weeks after finishing my time with the marines, an elderly lady screamed at me because I forgot her ranch dressing. When I was in college, I would have shrugged it off or calmed her down but not now. Now I had lost any ability to relate to people. I snapped. In my mind I saw myself punching her in the throat, killing her, and then standing over her body. I knew I was capable of doing it. I knew it could happen. My training had taught me how to turn that kind of aggression on but not off.

I was afraid of myself. There in the restaurant, I began crying, shaking, feeling the great surges of anger rise up within me as every pain I had ever experienced in my life just exploded to the surface. I backed off and looked straight up, aiming my words at God: "I can't do this anymore. Either I'm going to kill myself, or I'm going to kill somebody. You have to come down here. You have to take this."

As soon as those words left my lips, it was as if someone who had been standing on me simply got off. A weight was gone. Now, that scared me even more because I knew that it was God I had cried out to, and it was God who had just helped. What was I thinking? I was an alcoholic, an addict, a promiscuous man who was depressed and suicidal. Why would God help me? Didn't I deserve punishment, not rescue?

But rescue is exactly what happened. I was caught between homicide and suicide, but Jesus Christ found me. At the lowest, most broken point of a low and broken life, God heard my prayer and stepped in. Standing by the serving station, I felt my eyes fill with tears; I knew something had changed. I knew everything had changed. I just had no clue what to do next. How should I respond to a God I didn't know?

There was another server, a navy veteran, who would talk to me about Jesus from time to time. I told him what had happened, and that very night we went to another restaurant and talked. He told me about Jesus' life—the birth, the miracles, the teaching, and the death and resurrection. I was twenty-eight years old, and this was the first time I had ever heard the gospel. I knew it was what I had been searching for my whole life. I was at the end of myself, but that was the day my life began.

I was lonely, but I was not the only one. I know there are other people out there wondering if they matter, wondering if there is more to this life. Maybe you are one of them. Maybe you just need to believe that God has a plan for your life.

Over the weeks and months following that night in the restaurant, I discovered the freedom that comes from taking responsibility for my decisions, acknowledging and repenting for my sins, and accepting Jesus as my Savior. Jesus Christ has been next to you every step of your life, waiting for you to choose him and only him. In John 14:6, Jesus said, "I am the way and the truth and the life. No one comes to the Father except through me" (NIV). True life, eternal life, is found only in Jesus Christ.

TWENTY-NINE

Kissing My Wife Saved My Life

Gary Cropley

If ever there was a night we needed to take our wives out to dinner, it was this one. Through one of the strangest chain of events I've ever experienced, my friend and I had tracked and caught a kidnapper and would-be rapist and held him until the cops could take over. But hey, that's another story for another book. What matters to this tale is that both my friend and I were feeling thankful to God, not just for his protection during the hours that had just passed but for his provision of our two wonderful wives.

We were spending a weekend together that we had been planning for weeks. We were all excited about being in the middle of Oregon's wildest beauty. As well as the hiking, riding, and eating, we were looking forward to talking, laughing, and praying, then heading back home, reinspired by the love and grace of God and our good friends.

Our meal out that evening was everything we needed it to be, and as we drove back to the cottage, any remaining tension from earlier in the evening had lifted, and we were back to our normal selves. We were laughing at the old jokes and doing the old routines. I decided to celebrate the moment by pulling over and announcing that it was time to kiss our beautiful wives, which we did.

We all laughed as we pulled back onto the road, but within minutes the car was silent again. The road ahead— the very same road that we had driven down just a couple of hours before—was now completely blocked. All the way across was a wall of mud, at least fifteen or twenty feet high. The landslide had narrowly missed a house, from which a woman now came running.

"Are you folks okay?" the woman asked us. "It didn't hit you, did it?"

We must have looked confused because she stepped up to the car window and leaned in.

"It just happened—just a few seconds ago. You didn't see it at all? You didn't see the landslide?"

We were shocked. Had we not stopped for that kiss, we would have been by the house right when the landslide happened. We would have been buried under all that earth or forced off the road and down the mountain. Either way, I doubt we would have survived.

It took us an hour to detour our way back home, and somewhere along the way we met a road maintenance worker who told us just how big the landslide was. He asked where we were heading and if we would mind putting up a few warning signs when we got there. By the time we finally made it back, it was too dark and rainy to really see what we were doing. We grabbed the signs and stuck them in the first place we thought would give people adequate warning, then went home.

That next morning there was so much to talk about: the kiss, the landslide, and how close we had come to disaster. After breakfast we headed out to take another look at where the road washed away. As we rounded the final corner and got out of the car, we all stopped dead in our tracks. We could see the landslide covering the road, but where was the rest of the hillside beneath the road? It was gone—totally swept away. The landslide had been significantly more powerful than we thought, and it had left the road completely undercut. It was as if a giant had taken a mighty bite out of it, leaving nothing but a thin slice of pavement perched on an even thinner column of earth.

In the darkness and in our rush to get back to bed, we must have missed it completely. We must have turned the car around with only inches between the rear wheels and the gaping chasm of the mountain. How did we escape that one? And how close could we come to danger in just one night?

A few years on, and I'm happy to say, my weekends are much quieter. But I often think back to that kiss and encourage others to pay attention to those hunches and nudges of God. You never know what they might save you from and what they might lead you to. Sometimes they are obvious, sometimes not so much. And sometimes they let us be the rescuers while at other times it is we who are rescued. But whatever the outcome and whatever the plot, our God is always there, always calling us closer to him. Always.

THIRTY

God Meets Us Where We Are

Victoria Rodriguez

I was crying on my bed one day in late summer. My husband and I had argued a little before breakfast, and while he was out fixing the van, I told the kids to go play in their room because Mommy wasn't feeling well and needed to take a nap.

Lying on my side of the king-size bed, I watched my door creep slowly open. I saw my daughter's Chinese eyes peeking in to check on me. I waved her in with my hand and said, "Come on, baby. Come lie down with Mommy."

Amber came in, closed the door behind her, and crossed her way over to my side, cuddling her way into my arms. After some time, she spoke.

"Mommy, why are you crying?"

"Oh, baby, you know Mommy is a big crybaby."

"But why?" She wiped my tears. "Mommy, you don't have

to cry because I love you. I don't ever want you to cry or to ever be sad because I love you!"

Oh, my sweet baby! She had always taken care of me, always known the right thing to say at the right time. I gave her a big kiss and told her I loved her too. I lay back down, feeling warm inside.

When I finally left the room, Amber was there in the doorway, flashing me a grin from ear to ear with her two front teeth goofing out. She held out a piece of paper and said, "Here, Mommy. This is for you." It was a picture of two stick figures—me and her—and the words, *I love you. You are the best mom*, written above. I told her that I loved it, and she told me that she would hang it on the refrigerator so I would read it every day.

My husband and I made up, and we decided to go out to the river and barbecue. I sat on the love seat, putting on my shoes and listening as Amber and her younger brother, Toby, talked in the next room.

"Sissy!" he said. "I can't wait to die. I can't wait to die and go to heaven and be with Jesus. I am going to be sooo haaappy!"

"Nooo, Toby," Amber told her younger brother. "You're not gonna die; you're not gonna go see Jesus!" Then, as though bragging, she said, "I'm gonna go see Jesus first!"

A little puzzled by my crazy kids, I went out to the car.

During the forty-five-minute drive to the river, Amber told me about how she could not wait to eat the carnitas I was going to make. They were all excited, but Toby was soon asleep, snoring away while Rafa, the youngest, just played quietly in his seat. Amber held out for a while, but eventually she joined Toby, and in the rearview mirror I watched her fall fast asleep in the seat behind me, arms folded on the door, cushioning her head.

I made a complete stop at the intersection of Highway 46. There were no cars to the left, and only two or three far away to the right. As I slowly pulled out from the stop sign, I heard my husband call out, his voice heavy with fear, "No! No! No!"

I looked left, and all I saw were headlights. I looked forward again, gripped the steering wheel as tightly as I could, and floored the gas pedal, praying that the car would miss us and we would just fly over the road.

I woke up, still in the van. My husband was asking if I was okay. I nodded, and he jumped out of the vehicle, running around, yelling for our kids.

"Amber! Toby! Rafa!"

I felt a sharp pain in my neck and found it hard to move. Slowly, I shifted my body to the right and saw my Toby sitting there in his chair, covered in blood. He looked dazed, but he was coming to. Then I noticed that up above him, over the third row, was my son Rafa. He was dangling from his car seat. The impact must have busted his seat from the seat belt and flung him across the van, leaving him wedged in the back corner. I remember being confused, wondering how in the world he had gotten stuck up there. Then I noticed that the van's back door was wide open. *Thank you, God, for not letting him fly out of the back of the van.*

That was when I thought of Amber. At first I just called her name, but soon I was yelling it. I wasn't trying to wake her; I was grieving. I knew she was gone. I felt it.

A woman came to the car and tried to help me. I told her, "No, please, go check on my daughter."

She crawled her way to the back of the van to hold my daughter. Her son sat in the passenger side of the car, holding my hand, and I asked him to pray with me. I asked God to please not take Amber. I promised that even if she was sick, I would take care of her for the rest of my life. I pleaded with God, telling him that I could not live without her. My pleas rang out, and some bystanders told me to stop screaming. They said that Amber had a pulse, but I knew she was gone. I knew she was not coming back.

———————————

At the hospital I could hear Toby screaming somewhere nearby. I was desperate to find out what was wrong with him, and the doctor rushed in with news.

"Ma'am, he has internal bleeding, and we are going to rush him to emergency surgery."

I asked about Rafa because I could no longer hear him crying or screaming, and the doctor explained that they had just finished intubating him. He had bleeding on his brain, and if he made it through, he would probably have brain damage. *Please, Lord, don't take all of them. I know you have Amber now but, please, not all of them.*

The medication kicked in, and I started to drift away. Familiar faces of family members swept across my face. Soft voices told me it was all going to be fine. Louie, my ex—Toby's and Amber's father—arrived, and I told him Amber was gone. He said that I was wrong, that I must not think like that, and that he would go and check. I closed my eyes and prayed that I was wrong about her, pleading with God to change what I sensed had already happened. Time drifted. Prayers slowed. Then I heard Louie's voice, very soft and shaky, calling my name, "Victoria." I opened my eyes and saw both my husband and Louie on either side of me. My husband grabbed my right arm, and Louie grabbed my left. Louie said, "Amber didn't make it."

The days that followed are still a blur to me. I know I slept in Amber's bed, inhaling the only bit of her that was left in this world, wrapped in her covers, clutching onto the picture she had drawn me hours before she died, weeping until sleep took over.

By the time we buried Amber in the plot next to my grandmother, my boys had recovered fully from their injuries. Toby had suffered fractured ribs, a fractured jaw, and a torn spleen. Rafa had fractured ribs and a torn spleen, too, as well as bleeding on the brain. When Rafa came home from the hospital, he stood on the steps outside our house, stared up at the sky as if he was watching something, waved, and said, "Bye, Sissy!"

At some point I told my husband that as soon as I had woken up after the accident, I knew that Amber was gone. Whether it was a mother's instinct or the bond that I had with my daughter, I don't know. But I knew. My husband told me that Toby knew too.

"What do you mean, 'Toby knew'? How could he have possibly known that? He's only six years old."

My husband explained that as he carried him out of the vehicle, Toby had cried out, "Papi, I don't want to die! I don't want to die!"

"No, Toby, you are not going to die. Papi is here. The ambulance is coming. Don't you hear them coming?"

Toby told him, "But my sissy is dead; my sissy died already!" How could he have known that?

One night as Toby and I were driving alone, I started to talk with him. I asked him how he knew about Sissy dying. He glanced out of his window behind the passenger seat. I could see him thinking, remembering. Then, finally, he looked my way with a smile and said, "Because, Mommy, I saw her wings start to grow. They were baby wings and then grew into big wings. Not big wings but like her age wings." I was shocked. Then he said, "You know why Sissy died, right, Mommy?"

I replied, "No, Toby. Why?"

"Because, Mommy, Sissy wanted to save us. She woke us up from the accident because we were all dead." I took it in and remained quiet. I didn't know how to respond.

In the middle of October I invited my sister over for dinner. I made barbecued carnitas, Amber's favorite. My sister and I sat on the sofa, and she looked concerned as she spoke.

"How are the boys? Are they talking? Do they miss Amber?"

I told her that the boys were fine and that we talked about Amber all the time. I told her what Toby had told me the other week about seeing Amber's wings. I called him over, and he told my sister the same story. Just when I thought he was done, he looked down.

"But I was scared, Mommy."

"But why, baby? Why were you scared?"

"Because I saw the angels too."

I told him those were God's angels, and we don't ever need to be scared of them.

"Mommy, I was scared because I saw them taking Sissy, and I didn't wanna go. I wanted to stay here with you."

My sister and I looked at each other in awe.

Days later Toby and I were alone again, and I got to thinking about what he had said about the angels. So I asked, "Toby, remember how you said you saw the angels too? What were they doing? How many were there?"

He turned away and started pointing in the air right in front of him, as if he was counting. Then he looked back at me. "Six, Mommy. There were six angels."

I started picturing the six angels in the car and the five of us. It didn't make sense, so I asked, "Six angels? Man, that's a lot of angels. What were they doing?"

He shyly looked away and then placed his left hand on his left hip and said, "There were two right here." Then he placed his right hand on his right hip and said, "There were two right here." He grabbed his ankles—"One right here"— and then put his hand behind his neck and said, "There was one right here." He held out his left hand with his palm facing up, his right hand on top of it, also with his palm upward. "They all had their hands like this under Sissy, and they were going up, up, up, and up. And that's how I saw her wings, Mommy. They were coming out of her back, and it didn't even hurt her. And Sissy looked see-through, like Casper."

I was speechless again. My six-year-old son would never have known the significance of such a thing. Such a vivid vision could only come from God.

Not quite a year has gone by since Amber passed away, but so much has changed for me. I have become a better mother, a better wife, a better daughter, friend, and person. My encounter with my angel, Amber Brooke, has initiated my newfound faith. I have a new passion for life, and I have found a new way to love—through Christ.

I used to think that I could never survive the loss of a child. Now that it has happened to me, I can say that I have learned how to live through the pain. I have learned how to lean on God as I give my child back to him. It has changed everything for me, and I no longer fear life and all its challenges. Nor will I fear the Enemy and all his wickedness that lurks in the corners of every neighborhood.

Most important, I no longer fear death. I know that God reaches out to each of us, providing us with comfort and reassurance, reminding us that though the journey may be sudden or unexpected, at the end of our travels we will find ourselves with him, finally at home. I believe that is why he gave my little boy a last picture of his sister that he could understand and remember, one that he would later use to encourage me. I know that we are not angels, but even so, it still amazes me that God did what he did. He gave my little son a picture that he, with his childlike faith, could understand. The image of his sister growing angel wings sparked so much faith and trust in Toby that it sparked faith and trust in me as well. What God in his gracious kindness showed Toby changed everything.

THIRTY-ONE

Hurricane Omar

Emily Mayberry

I once had a catamaran in the Caribbean. We named her *Aeolus*, after the Greek ruler of the winds, and I never grew tired of staring back at her in some picture postcard cove. My husband, Vince, would listen to music in the cockpit while I swam out and snorkeled toward the pristine white beaches. For an unassuming country girl who grew up on a small farm, using an outhouse for the first ten years of her life, this was better than anything I had ever dreamed. With all forty-one feet of *Aeolus* beneath us, the world was my big blue ocean, and I was navigating it.

It was early October, and we were anchored in Simpson Bay on the Dutch side of St. Maarten, keeping a close eye on the weather reports. We were watching as a weather system named Omar developed into a tropical storm but were relieved to hear he was predicted to go northwest somewhere between Puerto Rico and the British Virgin Islands. Regardless of the report, boats were heading into the Simpson Bay Lagoon, a hurricane hole, for protection, and we decided to do the same.

Like many tropical storms, Omar refused to do what was predicted. Instead of turning northwest, he began a steady course toward the northeast and was soon upgraded to a hurricane. In time, the weather service issued a hurricane warning for the St. Maarten area with the storm due to hit within twenty-four hours. Thinking we were in a safer location, we settled down for the night.

The next day began with our usual ritual, waking up at sunrise and drinking coffee. Omar was still a good twelve hours away, but neither of us was happy with where we were anchored. *Aeolus* was in the middle of the lagoon, far too exposed and with no protection from the open water.

On land, we met Charlie—a friend of ours—at the Budget Marine store. He was purchasing more fenders for his catamaran—those white things that look like scaled-down punching bags and that stop the boat from smashing into the dock. We talked about the storm, and he suggested that we move to a mooring not far from him. It was a good idea, and we liked the idea of being attached to something solid—as well as having both our anchors down.

The weather can change so quickly in hurricane season, and even though the latest news told us that Hurricane Omar was due to miss us by fifty miles, we knew we were in for a big storm. We moved the boat to the spot Charlie had suggested, attached it to the mooring, and got busy securing everything we could.

We had planned on spending the night in a hotel onshore, but by the time we were done preparing *Aeolus*, it was already dark, so we stayed on board. We went to bed at 8:00 p.m., slept a little, and then woke up at midnight, ready to face the storm. We were prepared to leave *Aeolus* if necessary; our life jackets were close at hand, and I put on my fanny pack containing credit cards and cash.

At 1:00 a.m. I settled down on the couch in the salon and looked out the windows at the storm. The wind began blowing harder, and I saw the port-side fender blow up onto the deck. My nerves went up a gear. The next thing I saw was the front of the boat lifting up with the mooring chain almost horizontal. Great sounds of creaking and cracking could be heard from the front of the boat as if metal was straining against the powerful force of the wind and threatening to lose the battle.

I was frightened, and I asked Vince what was going on.

"We broke loose," he said. We were now completely at the mercy of the storm. Immediately we became airborne. I was sucked down under the salon table as *Aeolus* cartwheeled, bow over stern, and landed upside down in the water. Dazed by the move, I stood up and saw water rushing into the salon. Vince rose up out of the water and stood next to me.

"We have to get out of the boat," he yelled.

Down at my feet I could see the salon lights, giving just enough light to help get us oriented. Then they went out. Darkness surrounded us, but I could feel that the water was already up to my waist. We put on our life jackets, not knowing what kinds of waves were waiting for us out in the lagoon, but we quickly realized our mistake. In order for us to get to safety outside of the boat, we would not be able to float on the water, as our life jackets would force us to do; we needed to descend beneath the water. With the water already up to our necks, we scrambled to take off the jackets.

"Let's go. Follow me!" Vince commanded. He took three deep breaths and went underwater, exiting the boat from the cockpit area and under the stern.

I struggled with my life jacket, thinking I could carry it with me but finally let it go. *This could be it*, I thought as I took a deep breath. There was no panic, no fear of dying. I was calm as I went underwater and stepped out into the upside-down, fully submerged cockpit. I kept my eyes open, and I could see through the water as if I were in a lighted swimming pool. There was the white fiberglass of the cockpit floor over my head, and ahead of me was the familiar, hall-way-like opening that led out onto the port-side hull. I knew this was my fastest way out. I quickly swam over to it, then down under the hull, and toward the hull steps to get out.

It was dark out there, but I kept moving, struggling to get out as if I were in the birth canal all over again. I needed to breathe and struggled to fight the strong reflex that would have me open my mouth and inhale. I fought it with all my strength while, at the same time, frantically pulling, push-ing, and tearing myself toward the opening. Once, twice, three times I breathed in lagoon water, the pain in my lungs increasing with every second. Finally I felt my head break the surface, and I guzzled in air. What a welcome feeling! So simple yet so sweet.

I yelled for Vince and heard his voice coming from the middle of the overturned boat. I swam over to him and found him sitting on top of the bottom of the boat. He reached out and helped me up. I immediately began throwing up water. I was scratched, my clothes were torn, and I reeked of diesel fuel; but, thankfully, neither of us was injured. We heard voices from the marina and yelled for Charlie to come and get us. When he arrived in his dinghy, he was more welcome than any knight in shining armor. We were quickly off *Aeolus* and heading back to the marina and safety.

The next day we learned that the wind gust that had flipped *Aeolus* upside down was a tornado that had spun off Omar as he passed by St. Maarten. But that was not the only surprise. As we spoke with friends and retold the story of swimming out of the cockpit, Vince said, "It was dark. I couldn't see and had to feel my way out."

Surprised by this, I said, "Did you have your eyes closed? I could see through the water!"

In that moment I realized that seeing through the water had been a gift. The storm clouds had blocked out all traces of moonlight, but somehow I had been able to see; God had lit the way out of the darkness. Surely I would have drowned if not for the lit path. I had been spared.

A few days later as we left St. Maarten, our plane climbed into the sky above the very lagoon where *Aeolus* sat. She was broken, stripped of her mast and rigging, trampoline, and open-front canvas top, yet she seemed to glisten in the hot tropical sun, waiting to be transformed into something even more beautiful.

So much changed for me the night I nearly drowned. Like *Aeolus* herself, I was broken by the storm but given a chance to be remade—stronger, better. I needed to let go of the boat, to let go of the part of me that had made it an idol. I needed to open my eyes, trust God, and follow his light again.

I once had a catamaran in the Caribbean. Now I have you, my Lord.

THIRTY-TWO

The Check Is in the Mail

Ed Underwood

The hot Texas sun felt even hotter than usual as I struggled with the heavy railroad ties. We had just moved into a new rental house in Dallas, and the kind Christian landlord had offered to let me landscape the house in lieu of the first month's rent. And with our finances the way they were, we needed every bit of help we could get.

As a new student at Dallas Seminary, I had explained to this man and everyone else that it was just a matter of time before I would be generating an income stream. My first five-hundred-dollar monthly stipend from the GI Bill would be arriving any day, and I had a sure job through an old Young Life friend whose cousin owned an excavating business in the city.

But while I was confident that all would be well, time was running out, and my wife, Judy, and I were starting to wonder how long we could last. That "sure job" turned out to be no more than a flaky promise from a flaky cousin, and while rounding up our last quarters for a trip to the Laundromat, Judy voiced our fears.

"Eddie, what will we do? If we don't receive some money today, we won't eat! There's nothing in the house to feed the kids."

I reminded her of the GI Bill, said good-bye, and headed off to check on it at the seminary. Standing at the desk of the lady who assists veterans, I was told there was a problem with my account. As a veteran, I knew that when the government has a "record problem," it can take weeks or months to correct itself.

I returned home, feeling the weight of being stuck in Dallas without a job or friends and all out of options. Soon there would be no more railroad ties to move, and the next month's rent would be due. I began to doubt the decision to move here. What was I thinking, leaving a career I loved and a community that loved us? Our Officers' Christian Fellowship group in Ansbach, Germany, had become the closest circle of Christian friends we had ever experienced. The army had offered me command of a tank company as a first lieutenant. I could be leading Bible studies once a week and leading men on the frontier of freedom during the Cold War. But no, I had to follow my dream to come to Dallas Seminary. What was I thinking?

I heard Judy's car pull in and wondered how I could best break the news to her about the GI Bill. I felt like the worst husband and father who ever lived, and I was desperate for words.

She walked through the back door of our little brick

home with a glass of iced tea, and I remember thinking how beautiful she was. I felt a little ashamed; she deserved someone better, a husband who made wiser plans and would take better care of her. I also remember realizing how deeply committed she was to our Lord and our life mission.

"Did you pick up your stipend?" she asked with her *I hope you have good news for me* smile.

"There's been a . . . a mix-up. I had them scour their records three times, but my check just wasn't there." I looked back to the railroad ties, sensing her panic. Trying to sound optimistic, I continued, "The lady at the table for veterans said that she would try to track it down this week. So it looks like we're going to have to wait a few more days."

Judy was thinking exactly what I had thought to myself when I discovered there was a "slight problem." She had been a military wife long enough to know that there was usually nothing slight about paperwork mishaps.

God's Spirit used the panic on her face and the desperation in my heart to turn me toward him at that hopeless moment. "Sweetie," I said, looking into those drop-dead-beautiful green eyes, "I don't know what God has for us here in Dallas. But this I do know: Whatever happens over the next few years, there's one lesson I want us to learn. I want us to learn how to trust him more than we've ever trusted him before. What a tragedy it would be if, when I graduate in four years, I know a lot of Greek, Hebrew, and theology, but our little family doesn't know how to trust God at a time like this."

Judy smiled at me. I had seen that smile before, when she told me about how, as a fourteen-year-old girl, she and her brother and sister had been abandoned and sent to the children's ward in the local juvenile hall. As she thumbed through her Bible, desperate for something to tell her brother and sister, God turned her to Romans 8:28. Looking up, she told them, "We're going to be okay. God said so. He promises to bring good out of this. Mom's left us alone, but God hasn't, and I believe his promise."

Kneeling with Judy by the railway ties, I prayed. "Okay, Father. We believe that you led us here to this city and this neighborhood to attend seminary. We believe that this is your plan for us, and we're going to trust you, no matter what. Please help us. And please let us know that you're there. In Jesus' name, amen."

Judy added, "Lord, forgive me for doubting you. You've always been my only hope, and you're my only hope still. Please help us."

Too beat to carry on working, I joined Judy as she headed back inside. As soon as we walked through the back door, the front doorbell rang. I opened the door to a stranger who asked kindly, "Are you Ed Underwood?"

"Well, yes, I am," I answered a little suspiciously.

"I'm a fellow student at Dallas Seminary, and like you, I'm a veteran," he explained. "I picked up my GI Bill stipend today, and the lady noticed that your check had been misfiled. She felt bad that she had missed it, but then she realized that we live in the same neighborhood." He smiled, "If you're like me, you could use this right now. God bless, and welcome to the neighborhood."

As soon as I closed the door, I took Judy in my arms and was just about to tell her how much her faith meant to me when the doorbell rang again. It was the Western Union courier. "Are you Ed Underwood?" he asked. Suddenly it seemed that the whole world was looking for Ed Underwood!

I nodded. "That's me."

"If you could please show me some identification and sign here," he said cheerfully. I did as he asked, and he handed me an envelope. Closing the door, I turned to Judy. "It's from Frank and Cindy. I hope they're okay."

Frank and Cindy were a part of our close little fellowship group in Ansbach. They were now serving with the Twenty-Fifth Division in Hawaii, and we hadn't heard from them for quite some time.

I tore open the envelope, and something dropped to the floor. Judy grabbed it, and I read the letter they had sent: *We were praying for you and the Lord burdened us with a deep concern for your little family. Please know that we love you and we're so thankful for your friendship.*

"That was nice," I said. "I sure do miss those two."

Judy was frozen before me, staring at the piece of paper that had fallen to the floor. "Eddie!" She handed it to me and started to cry. I read the cashier's check, and then I read the numbers again to make sure I was reading it correctly: $2,000.00. It was a lot of money in 1980, and it was a fortune to us.

We had a worship service right there, jumping around the tiny kitchen of that little brick home in Dallas, Texas. Some people might call it all coincidence, but we knew better. It was—and remains to this day—one of the clearest indicators of God's personal care for our family. In a long history of God's caring for us, this one still stands out. We knew then, as we know now, that God's timing and provision are perfect.

We knew it was God who had caused the misfile of a government document and the correction that coincided with our praying in surrender to him. We knew it was God who moved the hearts of our dear friends to write a check and send it so that it arrived on the day he knew we would need it most. We knew it was God who had prompted the Western Union courier to plan his daily route so that he drove into our driveway at the perfect time. Through all this provision we heard God loud and clear. *I'm here,* he said. *Don't worry. Trust me.*

THIRTY-THREE

Safe

Stephen Jewell

I have been to some very dark places in my life. Though I know that I am a child of God and that he loves me, the darkness has often threatened to overwhelm me. I have often thought of taking my own life. But even though the battle still continues today, there is something different about the way I now face the struggle. I know that God still has plans for me. I know that I am not done yet.

Perhaps my darkest time was about a year ago. The battle had been raging harder than usual, and I was not doing well with my thoughts. I was alone in my house, alone in my head. The sense of being worthless was crushing me down, and the old temptation to kill myself dominated my every thought. Like a moth to a light, I could not resist. Upstairs in the gun safe by my bed was a pistol, and it was calling me to use it.

It might seem strange, but while I felt the irresistible pull of the gun, I also desperately wanted God to intervene. With each stair that I climbed, I called out to God to somehow stop me. As I neared the top, my cries grew louder, but still the gun pulled me toward it.

By the time I entered the bedroom, the battle within me was starting to show on my body. My legs felt as though they weighed a thousand pounds, and I could no longer walk. But though I believe now that God had heard my prayers and was answering them, it was not enough. Since I could not walk, I got down and crawled my way to the gun safe.

I pulled myself in front of the keypad and thought of the gun waiting on the other side. It promised relief—immediate relief from years of torment and pain. In just a few seconds it would all be over. Once I had the gun, I could finally be free. I concentrated hard on entering the code, blinking and wiping away the tears. I entered each digit in sequence and heard the internal bolt release. I reached for the handle of the safe and pulled, but the door would not open. I pulled harder, but it was stuck. Inhaling slowly, I entered the code again. Once more the sound of the bolt retracting told me that the safe was unlocked. And once more I pulled on the handle, but nothing happened. The door was jammed.

Was this God helping me? Was he somehow holding that door shut? I rolled onto my back and thanked God with all my heart. I knew he had saved my life. While I was praying, I heard a voice say, *I still have plans for you.* I knew then, for sure, that I had truly experienced a miracle. For several minutes I continued to pray, thanking God for saving my life and protecting my family from the pain caused by suicide.

Then the questions came. Was it truly a miracle? Did I really matter that much to God? Was I actually worth saving?

I thought of the safe and wondered about the bolt. Wasn't it more likely that, instead of God rescuing me from death, the batteries had just died? This was no miracle; this was just a coincidence. It was an accident, just like me.

I entered the code again. I heard the bolt move. I pulled on the door, and it opened. There were the pistol and a box of ammunition. But this time I was ready. It had nothing to do with the batteries, but everything to do with God. I had been saved. I was worth saving. He still had plans for me. I closed the safe and went downstairs.

This single event changed my life. It has not gotten rid of my depression, and I still have days when I feel worthless and question why I am here. But then I remember what happened. I remember the words God spoke to me: *I still have plans for you.* And today I know what those plans are. In fact, the plans God had for me were already there on the day he blocked my safe. Their names are Amy and Addison, my wonderful wife and my beautiful four-year-old daughter. They were the plans God had for me even though I couldn't see it clearly at the time. They need me, and I need them, and that makes all the difference in the world.

And there is one more plan God has for me—sharing my story and helping others into the loving arms of God. And who knows? Maybe this story is just for you.

THIRTY-FOUR

Hostage

Lisa Kamprath

On September 3, 2004, I was gathering donations from local businesses in my hometown. I lived in South Milwaukee, Wisconsin—a Mayberry-type town, full of mom-and-pop stores that have been in business for decades. The donations were for some friends at church who were struggling with medical bills after the birth of their first son. He had spina bifida, and I was confident this small town of mine would dig deep and help make our silent auction a success.

At about 10:30 a.m. I crossed the street for my first stop of the morning, Donn Powers Jewelers. I heard the door chime as I entered, and since the showroom was empty, I wandered a bit to look at some of the pretty baubles sparkling brightly under the lights. No one came out to greet me, but it was early in the morning, and the employees were probably still getting started back there. The empty space gave me time to rehearse my sales pitch again.

I heard a voice yell, "In here," from the room in the back. I ignored him, knowing that he would find me when he was finished with whatever he was doing back there.

A second time I heard him shout, "In here."

"It's all good," I shouted back. "Take your time." Suddenly a young man came through the doorway, and I was immediately struck with the thought that the dark T-shirt he was wearing didn't look at all professional. Still, I moved toward him and the chest-high counter that separated us both, held out my hand to shake his, and prepared to introduce myself and explain my mission. In my left hand I held my purse and my notebook, and as he cleared the counter, I noticed that in his right hand was a matte black semiautomatic gun. He had it cradled against him, and he grabbed my right hand with his gloved left hand. "You picked the wrong time to come in here," he said, pulling me through the doorway at the back of the shop.

My mind went blank, and I felt numb. In the back room I noticed that there were already four people on the floor as well as another young man with a gun. His gun was chrome plated, and he was much taller than the first gunman. He was also more aggressive and mouthy, swearing at us, trying to intimidate each of us. It worked.

I was told to lie on the floor with my hands behind my back. I am left-handed, so normally I put my left hand over my right, but this time I instinctively covered my left hand (and my wedding ring) with my right. As the first man duct-taped my wrists together, I heard him whisper that he was sorry.

As the five of us lay there and listened to these two young men stuffing jewelry into their black backpacks, I prayed but not for me. I was neither scared nor nervous. I knew that whatever happened, I was going home. I just didn't yet know to which home that would be. So I prayed that God would be with my husband and help him explain to our children—a six-year-old boy and three-year-old twin girls—why mommy had gone to be with Jesus instead of home to them. I prayed that God would embrace my parents as they grieved the loss of a child.

Suddenly the door chimed, and I heard a third man's voice as he entered the store. *Please*, I called out silently to the man, *don't try to be Chuck Norris. Please don't play the hero.* He was brought into the back room, where he tried to reason with the two thieves. It backfired, and the atmosphere changed. As a reward he and one of the employees had duct tape placed over their eyes so they could no longer look at the robbers.

Until this moment I had never understood the idea of tension being so thick you could cut it with a knife. But at this point the metaphor suddenly made sense. I felt over-whelmed by the tension, weighed down and smothered by it. With every second that passed, the men became more frantic to get out with their stolen goods. When they came in the back to ask for the surveillance tape, I felt they had to be nearly done. The female employee on my left told them there was no surveillance equipment. That left the six of us tied up in the back room as the only witnesses. The mouthy one said that since we all had seen their faces, he would kill us all. I honestly believed that he meant it.

I prayed fervently again. I prayed for my family and that my journey home would be swift. I heard the racking of both guns and waited for the first shot. As I wondered who would get the first bullet, the door chimed again. I remember screaming in my head to God, *Why are you bringing someone else into this terror? Why allow the evil to spread?* One man left the room—I couldn't tell which one, as I had my eyes closed and head down—and I heard the woman to my right beginning to say the Lord's Prayer aloud.

I heard a man's voice pleading from the other room. "I'll do whatever you want," he said. "Just please, don't hurt her." In my mind I saw a young couple coming in to pick out an engagement ring, and my heart broke for them. The tragedy was overpowering. As they were ushered into the back room, I opened my eyes just a little and glanced over my left shoulder. I saw two pairs of shoes: one belonged to a man, the other to a little girl. Through her sandals I saw that her toenails were painted bright pink. She couldn't have been much older than three.

The gunmen told her father to lie on the floor. They duct-taped his hands, but they did not touch the girl. They said nothing to her and left her alone. When they got back out into the showroom again, the little girl's father tried to stay calm for his daughter. He promised her chicken nuggets at McDonald's just as soon as they got out of the store. He said they would have balloons. When he called her *baby*, I thought of my own girls. I thought of my son, who would be turning seven in exactly one week. They all would have liked nuggets and balloons.

I again heard the two men talking in the other room. "I can't do a kid. We're done." Then the door chimed as they left. And that was it. We were spared. A child had saved us all.

While the police came and took our statements, I sat on

the floor, listening to the little girl talking about the third birthday party she had just enjoyed. She talked, and I smiled, the tension falling away from me with every exhalation. Before I left, I asked her name. It was Kaya. "It's a pretty name," I said.

"Yes," her father replied, smiling at me. "*Kaya* means life-giving."

THIRTY-FIVE

Faithful Provider

Beth Hopper

I knew I had made some bad choices, and the evidence was all around me. I was broke, alone, and six months' pregnant. My husband was out of state, trying to start a business, and in the transition we had sent our son to be with his grandma, fourteen hours away. With my family separated like this, I felt as though I was coming undone. I was desperate, and something had to change.

So I decided to get my son back. The only problem was, I was broke, alone, and six months' pregnant. Still, what choice did I have? I counted up my money, bought a ticket that would get me to my son on the other side of the state, and hoped that the five dollars I had left would somehow buy me enough food for the day's journey.

I hadn't been on the bus for long when a young lady with a little boy began talking to me. It was good talking to them, and it helped pass the time. Everything seemed fine until we stopped to eat at a bus stop. She asked if I could buy them lunch. I thought about the five dollars in my pocket. It was all I had. "Sure," I said. I warned her that I did not have much, but I would do what I could. The money was just enough for the three of us each to have a small cup of soup and some water. Before the bus carried us on, they thanked me and went their way. I walked back to my seat, thinking that I was going to be really hungry by the time I arrived at my destination, but I knew I had done the right thing.

Later in the day a girl got on the bus and sat beside me. She wasn't on it very long, and we never spoke, but at her stop, she got up and asked if I would like the lunch that her grandma had packed for her. I nodded, said thank you, and took the brown paper bag that she handed me. In it were a package of strawberries and a 7UP. They hit the spot.

We stopped again that evening for a dinner break. I got out to stretch and sat on a bench away from everyone else. My stomach growled, and I was impatient to get back on, but soon an elderly lady approached me and asked if she could share her Subway sandwich with me. She had gotten one that was too big, and there was no way she could eat it. Of course I said yes. I was very grateful!

I slept the rest of the trip, feeling content. Stepping off the bus, I was met by my dad. His first words?

"Do you want some breakfast?"

I gave so little—just a few dollars—and got so much back. I was amazed at how God met my need, how he cared enough even to give me my daily bread. In that moment I knew he would work out the rest of my situation as well.

THIRTY-SIX

My Cup Runneth Over

Kimberly Creech

When you are seventeen and about to go on your first overseas mission trip with eleven other friends, life feels pretty good. With high school behind you and college just around the corner, faith and optimism run high. Whatever the unknown adventure may throw at you, the Lord will provide.

That is how I felt back in the summer of 1998—the summer we spent two weeks sharing the message of Christ and making crafts in public schools in Brazil. And all those instincts were right: the adventure was wild, the optimism was well placed, and God really did provide. And how.

For two months before heading down south, our mission team had been scouring every supermarket and convenience store in the search of yellow plastic cups. They had to be yellow because we were going to use them, along with some string and sponges, to make little model chickens. Finding the cups was quite a chore when the only color that seemed to be available in stores was red, and Internet shopping wasn't anything like it is now. But we had been given the task of getting the cups, so we did not argue. We bought as many as we could find, finally maxing out at 750.

The first day in Brazil we organized our supplies: everything we needed for the chicken craft activity, some yarn for older children to work with, and some Portuguese tracts and New Testaments to be handed out on the street at night. Rio de Janeiro was a dangerous place to be, so once we had taken all that we needed for the first day's work, we stored the rest of the supplies in trunks with padlocks.

Day one of our mission work was a success. We saw almost seven hundred children, and with each one we talked about what Jesus was like, singing songs as we got on with the craft. They left at the end of the day with big smiles on their faces and yellow chickens in their hands. We were happy, of course, but our success introduced another problem. We still had almost two weeks remaining on our mission trip and only fifty cups left. We asked around, but nobody thought we would have any success finding more cups in the city. So what else could we do but pray?

As we closed up for the night, we laid hands on the almost-empty trunks, prayed, and then locked them up. We talked a little about some alternative things we could do with the children the next day, but mainly we prayed that God would help us by fixing the problem himself.

After breakfast the next morning we got ready for the day ahead, unlocking the trunks and loading up our backpacks with all the supplies we would need. Our youth ministers began handing out our rations, and it was only when all twelve of us had received all that we needed that we suddenly realized we all had the same amount as the day before. Somehow, instead of the trunks containing just fifty cups as they had the night before, that morning they were almost full again.

Day two was another success, and we saw as many new children as we had the day before. As the sun set, we returned to the trunks, saw them nearly empty, locked them, laid our hands on them, and prayed for God to fill them again. The next day those once-empty trunks had enough resources for each and every one of us to fill our bags, get out and preach the gospel, and show the love of Christ to the children. For the remainder of our two weeks in Rio, we prayed at the end of each night and opened the trunks the following day to find that we had more than enough to do our work. We twelve little evangelists were on a high!

As a child I had prayed to see big miracles, the kind that I read about in the Bible. I wanted to see people raised from the dead, seas parted, and loaves and fish multiplied. At seventeen I finally got to see 750 yellow cups and other supplies multiplied into enough for more than five thousand children. Thanks to God's provision, all the children we saw were able to take away something that reminded them of the day they heard about the man we call Jesus, who loves them more than anyone else ever could.

God did not have to provide in such a miraculous way, but he delights in giving us our hearts' desires. God blesses us with even more than we need, and not only did we have enough to use while we were there, but we were able to leave those trunks overflowing with supplies for the local missionaries to continue using after we returned home. What a loving God we serve!

THIRTY-SEVEN

Blind Faith

C. M. Osewalt

A headache that keeps a tough New Yorker from leading a service at his church is not your average headache, and mine was blinding me.

I couldn't see out of three-quarters of my right eye. Nothing helped, and by the time evening came around, I couldn't see out of my eye at all. My wife called a doctor friend.

What American doctor calls back on a Sunday night? Mine did, and within the hour I was in her office, in her hospital's closed wing, having an eye exam.

"You have a detached retina," she said. "I can't help you with this. I'm going to call a colleague."

At 7:04 a.m. on Monday I met Dr. Schubert. My right eye was in even more pain and swollen from the previous night's exam, and I felt a childish urge to keep my eye shut tight despite Schubert's constant admonitions to keep it open.

We battled. He won. Eventually he washed up and returned

to his throne behind his desk while I retreated to my chair. Holding a colored chart, he started telling me—in his rapid-fire, efficient German manner—exactly what was wrong with my eye.

"Well, you have six tears in your retina. It is completely detached. You have the tears here, here, two here. And the rest around here. If you had one tear, we would shoot a needle with gas in it and float the retina back in place. *Ja?*"

I nodded. This was all sounding far, far worse than I had expected.

"If you had two tears, maybe three, we would try to put a buckle in place. This buckle would hold the retina in place, but that will not work for you. Too many tears.

"So we need to operate, *ja?* We reconnect your retina back in place with eye surgery. You have extreme myopia in both eyes, so this operation will lead to cataracts and then scarring in a year, and you will probably be blind.

"So we are going with the third choice. *Ja?*"

"Hold it," I said. "You're telling me I'll be blind in a year after this operation?"

Dr. Schubert backed up a little.

"Probably . . . but you don't know. Perhaps. New methods are always being developed."

"Why can't I go for the buckle?"

"You see here? You have too many tears. It will never hold."

I paused. When I go out to restaurants, I always let the waiter or waitress order for me. I tell them, "Don't ask me what I want to eat; surprise me." So I asked Dr. Schubert what he would choose if it was his eye that was in trouble.

For the first time since 7:04, he paused.

"Well . . . I would go with the buckle. *Ja.* If it doesn't work, then I would have the complete reattachment surgery."

It wasn't what I was expecting. "If that is what you would do, why am I going with the reattachment surgery to start with?"

A longer pause.

"Well, I get a grade from the insurance companies after each surgery. If I try the buckle and then do the reattachment surgery, I get a lower grade, *ja?* The insurance companies want one surgery, not two, *ja?*"

At 2:30 p.m. I was in surgery to put the buckle in place. I had to be awake for the procedure, and despite all the pressure I could feel, it did not hurt like the previous exams. As I lay there, soaking up the force of the instruments, the black rainbows swirled, and I prayed. I prayed for a miracle.

I recalled a book on prayer I had read years before: *Beginning to Pray* by Anthony Bloom, a Greek Orthodox priest. In it he teaches about meditating on the prayer, "Lord Jesus Christ, son of God, have mercy on me a sinner."[*] I prayed each and every word, letting each one soak into my soul.

That night I was back home. I couldn't sleep and was still seeing rainbow colors. As I floated like Huckleberry Finn on the river, looking at the stars in a rainbow sky, the only sound was my voice echoing the Jesus prayer. I needed the mercy of God.

Tuesday at 7:00 a.m. I was back in Dr. Schubert's office, listening to his verdict.

"No. The retina has not attached to the buckle. Come

---

[*] Anthony Bloom, *Beginning to Pray* (Mahwah, NJ: Paulist Press, 1970), 60.

back Wednesday at seven. If it doesn't attach by then, we do a complete reattachment Friday, *ja?*"

I went back at 7:00 a.m. on Wednesday. The verdict had not changed.

"No. It has not attached to the buckle. Come back at seven, Thursday. I've scheduled the operating room for Friday."

Thursday, 7:11 a.m.: "No. Tomorrow we operate."

Before I left, I offered a final prayer: *Lord, if you want me to see, have mercy on me, Son of God.*

Dr. Schubert paused. "I want to try something." He took out two large needles. "I want to shoot gas into your eye. If the gas can float the eye back to the buckle, it might attach."

The pain was worse than any I had ever felt. Somehow I made it through. I left the room, beaten up and dazed as though I had just been taken down on the street. It was all I could do to let my wife guide me home. I prayed my prayer, my Jesus prayer, the entire night.

Lord Jesus Christ, Son of God, have mercy on me a sinner.

I am a spontaneous type of guy and usually pray in unfixed, moving words, out loud or silently, led by the Spirit. But there was something comforting about repeating these same words each moment. People have prayed this prayer for centuries. I was happy just to be with them, a pilgrim in prayer, asking for the miracle of undeserved mercy.

And I got it. The gas did the trick. The retina attached to the buckle. There were no more operations. I would have been blind, but instead I can see.

Finding out it had worked was not the last time I saw Dr. Schubert. There were checkups over the coming months, and every time we met he would remind me of how he had used an out-of-date technique in an operation not approved by medical insurance, with a less than 1 percent success rate, to restore my sight. Not only had the procedure worked, but the insurance company had paid up in full.

"You're a living miracle, *ja*!"

THIRTY-EIGHT

Our Gift from God

Dawn Liberski

My dream was peaceful, it was surreal, and it was simple. In it I dreamed that God told me that the baby growing inside me was a girl and she would have Down syndrome. He told me that she would be a blessing and that I should never worry. He told me that he would carry us through it all.

I woke up immediately. It had been two weeks since finding out I was pregnant, and even though it was 2:00 a.m., I knew I needed to share the dream with Darren, my husband. Sleepily, he told me that it was just a dream and he was sure everything would be fine with the baby. Darren went back to sleep, and I soon followed, hoping that God would be waiting for me in my dreams, ready to talk with me some more.

Days later at our first doctor's visit, I spoke of my concern about our baby having Down syndrome. On paper there was nothing to worry about, and the doctor reminded me that having my third baby when I was thirty years old did not place my child at any risk. But if it would make me feel better, he would do the triple-screen testing in a month or two and put my worries to rest.

Well, the week after the triple-screen test, I got a call to confirm that the marker came back high for Down syndrome. I felt so sad, and my tears were heavy. Our doctor wanted to carry out an amniocentesis to confirm or deny, and though I agreed to the test, I knew exactly what the results would be.

Once the diagnosis had been confirmed beyond all medical doubt—the same news that God had already revealed to me in a dream—we moved up the medical chain of command. A specialist took us on, and my little girl was scanned and checked multiple times. After what seemed like endless hours of lying in darkened rooms while ultrasound monitors hummed quietly next to me, we were told a little more about what was going on. As well as having Down syndrome, our baby girl had a heart defect and hydrocephalus, commonly referred to as "water on the brain." We were told that our little baby would not make it to term, and even if she did, the pressures of birth would be too much for her. The best thing we could do, according to the specialist, was abort.

We told him that we would never choose such an option and that God had given us this girl for a reason. We chose to never see that particular specialist again. Instead, Darren and I cried out to God in desperation. Our church continued to lift us and our baby up in prayer. God had promised to carry us through, and though we felt scared, we knew we could trust him.

On July 3, 2000, our miracle child was born. Though

Erica Lynn was born with Down syndrome, she had made it full term, made it through the birth, and showed no sign at all of any heart defect or hydrocephalus. Our little girl had been healed and was delivered to us just as God had told me she would be, eight months earlier in my dream.

I asked the doctor if he could explain her medical condition, but he could not. I told him that it was clearly a miracle, and when I finally had time to be alone with Erica in the hospital, I simply wept and thanked God for allowing her to be my child. I thanked him for giving me peace throughout the nine months I carried her. I thanked him for all the times I had been able to share my story of his love and care with others. And I thanked him that never once had I felt alone.

Erica was never a stranger to hospitals. She encountered problems with her lungs and her digestion, but on so many occasions we sensed—after we prayed—God clearly giving us wisdom and direction. And finally, in the last days of Erica's life, God answered our prayers. Just not quite the way we wanted.

One morning during those final days, Erica's night nurse greeted us as we walked back to see our little girl in her ICU room. The nurse told us that she had a story she needed to share with us. A little girl had been in a car accident that night and was being wheeled past Erica's room when she told the nurse to stop.

"Why are there so many people in white floating in her room?" the little girl asked, looking into Erica's room. The nurse knew that, apart from Erica, there was no one there.

Just hours after the nurse told us this story, Jesus took Erica to his home to be with him forever.

And true to his word, God had carried us all the way through, from the first dream about our special little girl, to the comfort of hearing another child's vision of seeing angels preparing to usher sweet Erica home.

THIRTY-NINE

Didn't You See Him?

Denise Meyer

We shoved away from shore, and I immediately took out my 35 mm camera. Round Lake, Wisconsin, is a beautiful place, especially when the weather is cold and the water is freshly thawed. We had rented a cottage by the water, and the little rowboat was a great addition to our wilderness experience. For the five of us in the boat—my two children (Emily, age four, and Tim, age two), my mom, my stepdad, and me—it was a perfect way to spend an afternoon. So what if we were one life vest down? What could possibly go wrong?

We hadn't drifted out more than fifty yards when I suddenly felt the boat rocking back and forth, making a wider swing with each rock. Dad was groaning in pain. His leg was cramping badly, and he was trying to stand up in the boat. Mom screamed at him, "Will, sit down! *Sit down!*"

I dropped my camera and grabbed the sides of the boat just as the momentum of the final swing tipped the boat completely over, thrusting us all into the cold water. With no time to catch a breath before going in, I came up gasping for air. Having been trained in water rescue by the local fire department just a few months earlier, I knew I had to count the number of people who had surfaced. *Start counting and make sure everyone is up. One. Two. Three.* My parents had surfaced but not my two kids.

Dad—who had lost an arm in a car accident years before and could not swim—hung on to the capsized boat, his life vest keeping him afloat, while Mom and I searched frantically for the kids. I pushed my face down into the water, my bones penetrated by the cold. With teeth chattering and body shaking from head to toe, I could not see much in the murky water and soon had to come back up for air. I started crying and praying, *Please, God, don't take my kids! Please don't let them die!*

I threw my head back under and searched some more, my arm waving around blindly, desperate to find them. At last my hand caught hold of something familiar, but which child was it? Whether it was Emily or Tim, I could tell that the child was caught under the boat, the life vest pressing him or her upward into the frame. I tried to pull the child out, but I was out of breath. I resurfaced to hear my mom yell to me, "I found her! I have her foot! I have Emily!" With renewed determination, I pulled on Tim's leg, using my arm as a lever. I heard Emily surface, choking and crying. I pulled and pulled, but nothing was working.

It must have been going on ninety seconds since we capsized, and I had no idea if I would pull a lifeless baby son out from the water or not, but I had to give it one last pull. I prayed, *God, please, help me get him out!* In the pain of pushing my forearm against the steel edge of the boat, I pulled on Tim's vest with every ounce of strength left in me. Suddenly something gave way, and he popped out and up. He was choking and screaming, but he was alive! We were all alive.

In the moments that followed I became aware of what was going on around the lake. Everyone was looking our way, and I saw my brother-in-law jump into a boat that was tied to a pier, pulling away so fast to reach us that he brought part of the pier with him. As I watched people come to us and take us back to the shore, I realized afresh how cold the water was and how close we had come to death. And as we made it onto land, I learned how God had miraculously intervened.

Tim had been under the boat but in an air pocket. The only time he had spent with his face in the water was when God had given me the strength to pull him down and out. This was just sinking in when I heard another frantic cry.

"Someone call the ambulance! This woman is having a heart attack!" My mom was lying down on the dock, and I knew that I was seeing a second miracle in action. Had the heart attack started when we were in the water, she would surely have drowned.

But God was not done with us even then. There was another miracle still to be revealed, and we learned about it later that day when we were allowed to join Mom at her hospital bedside. Once the kids had fussed over their grandma for a time, the conversation turned to the accident on the lake. The fear returned to Mom's face as she spoke.

"Oh, Emily, I was so afraid when you were in the water. I

looked and I looked, but I couldn't find you. Then I reached out and grabbed you and pulled you up."

Emily looked confused. "Grandma, didn't you see the man?"

"What man?" Grandma asked.

"Grandma," she continued with a most serious look on her face, "the man under the water! He grabbed my foot and put it in your hand!"

Not yet getting it, Mom tried to explain, "Emily, there was no one else in the water with us."

Not giving up, Emily insisted, "Yes, there was! There was a man! He found me and gave my foot to you!"

We owe everything to God as he spared our lives and gave us more time to rejoice together as a family. Too often we are quick to assume that God has left us to fend for ourselves when we are in a crisis. We had seen not just one miracle that day but three; and out on the lake we all were reminded that not only is God with us when we face trials, but he is also at work in ways we cannot even see.

FORTY

Miracle in the Mail

Kimberly Donaldson

They say that a loved child has many names. My grandfather—William Degnan, Bill, Grandpa Bill, Dear Old Dad, DOD, Grandpa Knothead—was known and loved by many people. He was a strong, intelligent man, and on the day he died, I felt overwhelmed by guilt.

Nearly seven years ago he was in the hospital for his eighty-sixth birthday. It was a Friday. His daughter—my mom—had crossed the country from Arizona to visit us, and she sat alongside my husband and me as we sat beaming from our seats on the first night of our daughters' dance recital. I wanted to call Grandpa Bill, to wish him a happy birthday and find out how he was doing down there in Arizona. Mostly, I wanted to talk to him about eternity. Mom had told me his time was running out, and this was one conversation I did not want to put off.

Somewhere between the busyness of the hours leading

up to the show, the distractions of life with a young family, and the disobedience that thrives when emotions run high, I didn't phone. Time got away from me. I allowed the call to be squeezed out of my Friday, out of my Saturday, and out of my Sunday. On Monday I wrote him a note so that I could include some pictures from Bailey and Abby's dance portraits and recital. I included the regular goings-on type of information. Yet again I wrote as best I could about God's love for him and his plan for salvation. But I didn't call.

On Tuesday the mail left our mailbox, carrying my letter from rural Pennsylvania, beginning its two-thousand-mile journey all the way down to Arizona.

On Wednesday the phone rang. It was my mom. Grandpa Bill had passed away Tuesday evening.

My letter. It was too late. I felt as though all the breath had been sucked out of me. Why had I waited? Why had I pushed aside the urge to call him? Why had I not pushed aside the busyness, worked through the distractions, or overpowered the disobedience and called him? The guilt was heavy and served to intensify the grief. Later that day, having spoken and prayed with some friends, I realized that although I had missed the opportunity and the blessing of that conversation, my grandfather's response was his own. I was not responsible for his salvation; he was.

A couple of days later during a phone call, my mom said she had warned my grandfather's friend who had been with him at the hospital that a letter from me would be arriving there soon. His friend said that she would go collect it, although, emotionally, she might not be able to handle another sweet letter from me. She said that if it was anything like the one she and Grandpa Bill had looked at Tuesday evening—with such beautiful photos of the girls all dressed up—it might just be too much to bear right now.

She was talking about the letter I had mailed on Tuesday. It was the only letter I had mailed to Grandpa Bill, and nobody else had sent him photos of my girls—or of any of the grandchildren. I was ecstatic and spellbound. The letter I never imagined could have made it in time had traveled all the way from Pennsylvania to Arizona in a single day, thanks to the US Postal Service and a miraculous act of God! If the Spirit of the Lord transported Philip from one place to another (Acts 8:39–40), I guess speeding up the delivery of a letter wouldn't be that hard for God!

What a gift—for both my grandpa and me. I hope that at the end of his days, in his final hours, Grandpa Bill truly placed his faith in Jesus Christ. I hope that he experienced a blessed homecoming, walking into the arms of his Savior.

As for me, God showed me that he invites me to be a part of his plan. He does not need me to do it, and his purposes are not dependent on me. When I am obedient and sensitive to his leading, I can join him in his mighty work. I can experience the fulfillment found in an active relationship with him. I can bring glory and honor to him. I can share in his blessing. As Isaiah 55:6 says, "Seek the Lord while He may be found, call upon Him while He is near" (NKJV). Today, not tomorrow or next week, is the time to call on him and respond.

FORTY-ONE

The Day God Flew
My Airplane

Donald Seybold

I had had emergencies before. With one thousand pilot hours behind you, it is impossible not to have experienced what it is like when things go wrong. But I had never experienced anything as complex or as far outside the trained emergency procedures as this. Nothing at all.

The flight from Kadena Air Base in Okinawa, Japan, to Naval Support Facility Diego Garcia (affectionately known as Dodge, after the last outpost in the Old West) was a long one. But it was also supposed to be routine. The plane had just been through some major maintenance, and it was my job to safely deliver the four-engine propeller aircraft, called the P-3 Orion, to the Naval Support Facility in the middle of the Indian Ocean. The journey would take more than eighteen hours, so we planned to stop overnight at a remote air base in Thailand. For my crew, an overnight stop in Thailand was compensation enough for the boredom of the flight.

Only one hour after we left Okinawa, there were indications in the flight station that something was wrong. It was not a major problem, just a green warning light indicating that one of our engines may have clogged fuel filters or contaminated fuel. It would need to be checked over once the aircraft landed. Knowing that the air base in Thailand did not have the facilities to run the required maintenance, I made the decision to divert to a navy airfield in the Philippines. I informed the crew and altered the course. If all went well, we still would be spending the night in Thailand.

So far, so good. The flight progressed without incident, and the engine did not seem to be troubled by the fuel. It was probably a malfunctioning sensor, but we needed to get it checked out. The approach to the runway was unremarkable, but when the aircraft touched down, our world began to unravel. As soon as we made contact with the tarmac, the number three engine stopped operating, an occurrence known as a flameout or an uncommanded engine shutdown. With three remaining engines still working, I wasn't too concerned, but I knew that because of the design of the airplane, it would take longer to stop.

You see, the P-3 lands at a typical speed of 130 miles per hour. To get that down to zero requires reverse engine thrust—the propellers blow air out in front of the aircraft. But before we were able to complete emergency shutdown of the number three engine, the engine gauges on the number two engine indicated another flameout. And as if that weren't enough, the number four engine flamed out at the same time. Now I only had one working engine and no real way to stop the airplane. I had no control of the P-3 and could see, traveling at more than one hundred miles per hour, it was only a matter of seconds before we left the side of the runway and crashed down the thirty-foot embankment and into the ocean below.

We were doing everything we could to stop the airplane by using the remaining brakes, but with only the number one engine producing reverse thrust and ground control steering lost, the aircraft began veering to the left side of the runway. All I could see from my side was a sloping bank, a road, rocks, and water. Above the noise of the engines, I could hear my copilot yelling that we were all going to die. Honestly, I was feeling the same thing, but I commanded him to stand on the right brake as hard as he could. The flight engineer was going through all the emergency procedures in the hopes of restoring the brakes and ground steering, and I had so much adrenaline that I actually broke the cable to the nose wheel steering that was locked without control. Still, there seemed to be only one possible outcome, and that was almost certainly going to result in the destruction of our plane and possible death. And then I heard a voice telling me to add power.

None of our military emergency procedures called for adding power, and we certainly could not gain enough thrust to take off again. All of my senses told me to ignore this advice, and so, putting it down to panic, I put the thought out of my mind. But then it came again. *Add power.* Suddenly I realized it wasn't my inner panic, but it was God telling me to add power. I did what I was told, throwing the power lever to full power on the one remaining engine. And as I did this, the aircraft returned to the runway, where the brakes were able to work, bringing us to a complete stop on the centerline, twelve hundred feet from the end of the runway.

Thirteen of us were saved that day, and I know it was God who lifted my airplane back onto the runway. Like many Christians, I wanted to be in control and fix the problem myself. I wanted to keep the power. Only when I gave up and submitted to the Lord were we truly back in control again. Adding power was not about engines and fuel; it was God's power that made the difference. Surrendering to him, choosing to trust and obey him, was all it took.

FORTY-TWO

The Reluctant Missionary

Bruce Broyles

The truth is I was never really all that sure that I should have gone there. In fact, I did not even want to go. But everybody else told me that it would be a great experience. "You should go," they said. "It'll be good for you." But watching that little girl run off in tears, hearing her screams echo down the corridor, I began to think that they were wrong and I was right; I really should have stayed at home.

We were in St. Petersburg, Russia. There were sixteen of us from Ohio that my childhood friend, who was now a pastor, had brought to help a group called Russians Reaching Russians. It is an annual thing, and when my friend's wife found out she could not make the trip, he asked me to go. I couldn't say no, but I didn't exactly give a big yes either. I made little to no effort to raise money for the trip and applied late for my passport, but just when it looked as though there was no way I was going to make it, someone donated one thousand dollars toward my trip, and my passport came back within two weeks. While the other team members had been buying items to take with them and give to the trainee Russian pastors, I had bought nothing and had no money left. But when someone gave me fifty dollars, even I had to admit that it seemed as though things were coming together. My wife and I went to a store and bought as much as we could with the money, and just before checking out, I picked up a large packet of marker pens. I was finally ready to go.

Only I really wasn't ready. When we arrived, I was feeling out of touch and out of place. Everyone else was able to quickly make strong connections with the people there, but not me. I could not even seem to do a simple, nice thing, like give away that five-dollar pack of marker pens. I was walking down a corridor, looking for someone to give them to, when I saw a little girl walking toward me. I handed them over, and she took them, but she immediately started sobbing and then ran away. What had I done? Had I committed some kind of major social blunder?

I was still standing there, feeling sorry for myself, when the little girl returned. This time, she was with her father—who spoke very little English and was looking for one of the translators—and she was not crying anymore. Actually, she looked happy. The interpreter showed up and explained that everyone knew that her older sister really liked art, so she had already been given paper, pens, pencils, and more. The little girl had been hoping that she would receive some, too, but she hadn't so far.

Her father had told her to pray about it. He had told her

that God would see that she received what she needed. And he did. That was what her tears and screams were about.

I had come a long way to be used by God to answer a little girl's prayer. And it felt good.

FORTY-THREE

The Man in the Suit

Jamie Schull

*Jesus, either save me or take me now. Please, Jesus. Either save
me or take me now.*

I was upside down in my car, which—after I had lost control of it on the road above—had come down the bank and
was now lying on its roof in a river runoff area. The sunroof
had been knocked out in the accident, and the car had quickly
filled with cold March water. It was dark down there and so
cold. Trying as hard as I could, I was able to unbuckle my belt,
but I had no such luck when I tried to open the automatic windows and doors. As far as I could tell, I was trapped. I searched
desperately and found a pocket of air just enough to stick my
nose in and breathe. I felt my heartbeat slowing down, and
that's when I remember praying, *Jesus, either save me or take me
now. Please, Jesus. Either save me or take me now.*

Even though the water was painfully cold, I felt a sense of
warmth and peace come over me after I prayed. And I felt a

strong sense that, at eighteen years old, my life was too short to be over. I suddenly heard someone talking, felt some of the water escape, and saw light come in as the door opened. I saw two men: one, a young black man, and the other, an older white man in a black suit. The young man stood on the bottom of my overturned car, reached down and in through the door, and pulled me up and out.

I saw a crowd of people standing on top of a hill next to an ambulance. I felt someone next to me, wrapping a blanket around my shoulders. People asked whether I was hurt. I looked around again for the two men, but the old man in the suit was gone.

In the hospital, where I was treated for hypothermia, I found out later what had happened. The young guy who pulled me out—Anthony Pride—thought he saw a car upside down in the river bottom. He convinced his dad to stop, made his way downhill, and climbed onto the bottom of my car to see if anyone was alive inside. Anthony Pride could not swim, but he managed to get the door open and pull me out. I asked the police officers, who had come to the scene, about the other man, the one in the suit. Who was he? Nobody else had seen the man, and I was left thankful but a little mystified.

The mystery got only deeper when I went to the impound lot to see if there was anything I could retrieve from the car. My doors were stuck, locked, and buried halfway up in silt and mud from the river bottom. The people at the lot had no idea how anyone could have opened the door by hand.

A year later I was visiting with my grandmother when she decided to get out some old photographs. For some reason I don't think I had ever seen a photo of my grandfather.

All I knew was that he had died of a heart attack when my father was fourteen years old. He was only thirty-eight when he died, and my dad had talked to me about him occasionally when I was a little girl. My grandmother pulled out a photo and handed it to me.

"Here he is in his army uniform when he was a young man."

I was in shock. I did not remember ever having seen this—or any other pictures of my grandfather—but I recognized him instantly. He was the man in the suit who had been there on the day of my accident. There was no doubt about it in my mind.

I know that God showed Anthony my wreck and gave him the courage to save my life. I know he sent my grandpa to help. And I know that God kept me here because he was not done with me. Today, as a mother of five beautiful children, I know beyond any doubt the truth that lies within these wonderful words of Scripture: "We know that God causes all things to work together for good to those who love God, to those who are called according to *His* purpose" (Rom. 8:28 NASB).

FORTY-FOUR

Do Not Be Afraid

Megan McClowry

April 15, 2013, was supposed to be a joyous celebration for me. It was a chance to test myself, to compete alongside thousands of others as we ran in the most prestigious US marathon. I was looking forward to pushing myself hard and setting a personal best on a hilly course. But while some may remember the times they ran for that year's Boston Marathon, it was the horrendous loss of life that marks the event more than any personal record. And for me, it was the day I experienced God's physical protection in a powerful way.

Let me start at the beginning. My goal for Lent that year was to follow a reading plan that took me through Scripture. Like my training for the marathon, my reading had gone well, although as I approached the weekend of the run, I somehow got behind. So as I prepared to go to sleep on the Sunday night before the race, I read what I should have read the day before: Psalm 27. Even though I was behind, I still cherished the words that David wrote:

> The LORD is my light and my salvation;
> Whom shall I fear?
> The LORD is the strength of my life;
> Of whom shall I be afraid? . . .
>
> Wait on the LORD;
> Be of good courage,
> And He shall strengthen your heart;
> Wait, I say, on the LORD! (vv. 1, 14 NKJV)

I smiled. What better reading could there be for a nervous runner just hours away from the start line? Little did I know how fitting it really was.

I had finished four months of training, and the marathon morning (known as Marathon Monday) was finally upon me. I made it to the holding area in Hopkinton on time and found a spot in the grass to read and relax for two hours before the race. I had my hood up to shield me from the cold and my head bent down over my magazine when a random woman came up behind me, kneeled down, put a hand on my shoulder, and said, "Can I ask you a weird question?"

"Sure," I replied.

"Well, you may think this is weird, but can I pray over you?" she asked.

"Yes. Actually, I am wearing a rosary," I said, pulling up my sleeve to show the red rosary that I was wearing as a bracelet wrapped around my arm. The lady's facial expression didn't change, as though the fact that I was a Christian wasn't news to her. She simply put her arm around me and prayed.

"Lord, I ask that you protect Megan as she runs. Keep her safe, and give those legs of hers enough strength to finish the race. Don't let any leg cramps get in the way. In your name we pray. Amen."

I thanked her, and as she walked away, I turned around to see whom she would pray over next. But I could not see where she had gone; it was as if she had disappeared. I was puzzled. Who was she? Why did she come up to me? How had she known my name? She was wearing neither running clothes nor a volunteer jacket, and the gear bag with my name on it was not easily visible. I have run hundreds of races, but never has anyone asked to pray over me. Still, I was grateful that she did.

I made my way to the start line, putting my rosary in the pocket of my shorts as I walked. As the starting gun went off and I waited for the sea of people around me to start moving, I joined three random girls behind me in saying a prayer to the Lord. And then we were off.

The race went well. I stuck to the pace I had been training for, and several times I said silent prayers to the Lord, repeating the verse about how I can do all things through Christ who strengthens me. It all helped me get through the run. After twenty-six miles I was finally turning onto Boylston Street, taking in the cheers of spectators and the sight of the blue-and-yellow finish line up ahead. With my watch showing 3:25:17, I crossed the line. It was a personal best, and I pulled the rosary out of my pocket and held it up for my finish line photo. God had seen me through.

I continued to make my way through the finish line area when a volunteer told me I looked pale and wheeled me to the medical tent. I stayed there and rested but after fifteen minutes felt well enough to leave. I got my gear and began texting my family, who were back in a restaurant two blocks from Boylston Street, near mile twenty-six. I told them to stay where they were and I would meet up with them later. My mom texted me back: *ok, we are so proud of you.* That would be the last I would hear from them for several hours.

The moment the bombs went off was the moment that all the happiness and pride I had been feeling suddenly vanished. It was as if the noise of the blasts blew nothing but fear and confusion into everyone standing around me. Eyes wide, hands over mouths, spectators running, runners standing still, some crying—it all turned upside down in that instant. As ambulances and sirens filled the streets, I felt the overwhelming need to know where my family was and whether they were safe. But what should I do? What if there was a third bomb? Where could I find safety? My cell phone could not get through to them, and for two hours I did nothing but walk, aimlessly searching for them. I finally found out they were safe, and in time, I was able to give my mom and sisters the biggest hug as we reconnected at our hotel.

That night as I responded to messages from concerned friends and family back home, I read a text from one of my friends who is a Holy Cross sister. She told me that she had said a special prayer for me that day, and it reminded me of the woman who prayed for me as I waited for the race to start. Both their prayers had been answered; my legs stayed strong enough to get me through the course faster than ever before, and I was kept safe from the danger that lurked in the crowd around the finishing line. Had I stayed in the medical tent for another thirty minutes, I would have been just steps from the bomb blast. I slept that night knowing that God had protected me in mighty ways that day.

The next morning I opened up the gospel reading for the day. It was John 6:30: "What sign will You perform then, that we may see it and believe You?" (NKJV). God was right. I did not need to be afraid; he had sent a guardian angel to me that day. If ever I needed a sign that he loved, protected, and cared for me, I had it loud and clear.

FORTY-FIVE

A Handful of Change

Jessica Reyes

I needed to get from New Jersey to my home back in the Bronx. It was going to take two buses to get me home, and after paying for my first fare and finding a seat by the window, I soon realized that I did not have any money to pay the second fare. I had no ATM card with me and no other way of getting ahold of some cash. In my head I filed through the potential options. Maybe I could take a cab and have my mom pay for it when I got home. But what if she wasn't home or didn't have the money? Maybe I could explain my situation to the next bus driver. Would he let me ride for free? A free bus ride in the Bronx didn't sound like the kind of thing you could pin your hopes on. I was all out of options.

So I started to pray. I began talking to God as you would talk to a friend or a parent. *Lord, I need to get home, but I have no money. I know that it says in your Word that you will provide. So I have no idea how or where you are going to find provision for me, but in light of your promise, I present this need to you.*

I tried to put the problem out of my mind as my journey continued, but as we pulled into the bus terminal in New York, I started to worry again. Instead of praying some more, I went back to trying to find my own solution. What if I checked out those public pay phones right in the middle of the terminal? People are always leaving coins in there, and there must be fifteen machines for me to check.

I stopped. Before making a fool of myself by pressing all the coin return buttons and checking in the little metal trays, I wanted to make sure I knew exactly how much money I needed. A quick tour of the darker corners of my coat pockets revealed a crumpled receipt, a gum wrapper, and $1.25. Good. All I needed was another dollar.

I began counting my change again, just to double check, when my counting was suddenly interrupted by a voice in front of me.

"Excuse me . . . excuse me, Miss. Do you need change?" I looked up, and to my surprise I found myself face-to-face with a man I perceived to be homeless. His hair was unkempt, and he was wearing a long black heavy winter coat even though it was way too warm for it. In his left hand was a beer, and in his right was a fistful of change that he was waving at me.

I froze. My natural instinct was to turn him down. I mean, how can you take money from a homeless person? Didn't he need it far more than I did? But remember the prayer. Remember that you asked God, right? You asked him for help, and here it is.

Again the man asked me, in slurred speech, "Do you need change?"

"Y-Yes," I stumbled. "But I only need a dollar."

"Nooo!" he said, waving his fist again. "Please, take it all."

"No, sir. Thank you, but all I really need is another dollar to complete my fare." He opened his hand, held it out to me, and told me to take whatever I needed. And so I did, thanking him for his kindness.

"Good-bye," he called out as I walked away. "And God bless you."

All the way home, first on the bus and then on foot for the final minutes, I felt as though I were floating. I thanked God again and again, then praised him and thanked him some more. God loved me, and he cared for me even in the most insignificant of situations. Isn't that just like God, to reach down and help? And he was not just teaching me to trust him, but at the same time he was helping me to see people as he does.

My miracle encounter did not involve a miraculous cure or a divine vision, and it was not about finding myself in a place of danger or tasting the bitterness of grief. But even today it still reminds me that God helps us with even the smallest of our troubles and that he listens to us even when we fear he won't. And most of all, it is a story about God's beautiful, irrepressible sense of humor, and the wonderful ways in which he turns our assumptions upside down.

FORTY-SIX

Redeemed

Paul Holway

When you are a ten-year-old boy and you want to find a way to escape the pain that burns like acid within you, you look for release in the strangest places. Some choose to bully their classmates. Others choose to torment their teachers. I chose a different and much more dangerous path. My rage and pain went far too deep for easy release, and I soon would ruin a part of my life and that of many others forever.

I was born and raised in a Christian home in Gunnison, Colorado. We attended church every Sunday, and I learned about God and read all the stories in children's church. I had two parents at home as well as an older brother and a younger sister. My dad, a devout believer, was very involved at church and was often gone because of church-related events. I regularly saw him, though, praying in the mornings when I got up. My childhood, as my family, appeared as normal and healthy as any other.

But in the same way that I did not know anything more about Jesus than the stories in the books, I barely knew my father. My mom, though, I knew far better. I knew the way my skin stung when she first spanked me and how the red patch of flesh would turn into the beginnings of a bruise the next morning. I knew the feeling of fear rising inside me during the thirty-minute bus ride home on the days I had gotten into trouble at school; mile by mile, minute by minute, I became increasingly scared to face her. Not surprisingly, I had started acting out in school and was sent to the principal's office regularly.

I was pretty short and heavy when I was ten, and I guess I was an easy target for bullies. Unable to defend myself, I just soaked up the abuse. Unable to talk to anyone, I seemed to have no other choice but to stuff all my feelings down inside. Unable to exercise any kind of power or control over my life, I started to hurt and kill small animals. They could not defend themselves any more than I could.

I was mad at everyone, but most of all I was mad at God. Even though I really did not understand or know who God was, I knew it was his fault. I hated him for taking my dad away and taking up all his time. I didn't fit in with my family, and I didn't fit in at school. I was a loser, and my self-hatred became stronger and stronger. I began thinking of ways to kill myself. When the school bus dropped me off, I would think about lying under the tires so the bus would run me over. When out rock climbing, I would stand at the edge of a cliff and think about jumping and ending it all. But I was too scared to go through with any of it, which makes what happened next even more inconceivable.

On November 17, 1988, I was twelve years old and going through yet another miserable day. I had gotten into a lot of trouble at school that day, and I knew I would be in even more trouble when my mom got home. While on the bus ride home, I tried to think how I could possibly avoid the punishment I had coming. I had so much fear and anxiety about facing my mom, but what could I do? I couldn't run away; I had nowhere to go. Finally I came up with a plan that would make everyone forget what I had done at school and make sure my mom never touched me again. The plan was unfathomable and still makes me shudder twenty-five years later. I decided to shoot my little sister, Bethany.

As soon as I was home, I loaded my dad's hunting rifle and went into her room. She was playing and, when she saw me, asked what I was doing. I didn't say anything. She didn't even see the gun. I pointed it at her, pulled the trigger, and shot her. Immediately after the gun went off, I panicked. My ears were ringing from the noise of the gun, and I still remember the strong smell of gunpowder. After running all through the house, screaming and crying, my only thought was to call my mom at work. What I had just done seemed to come and go. One minute, it was so real; the next, it felt as if I were dreaming. My thoughts and feelings were so scattered. After what felt like an eternity, the EMS, the police, and my mom came running through the door. The paramedics put Bethany in the ambulance and left for the hospital. My mom drove our car, following the ambulance. All she kept saying to me was, "Why did you do it?" and "You need to pray that she lives."

Bethany died on the way to the hospital. She was only eight years old.

That night I was put in the county jail. I remember my dad stayed with me so I would not be alone. Having him there in my cell provided a source of comfort, but comfort could help only so much. Killing Bethany had removed something from inside me. It felt as though part of my soul had been ripped out. I cried that night until I had no more tears to shed. I was later sentenced to juvenile life—a five-year term—and my heart hardened even more as my hatred for life grew.

Years later my mom told me that on the day I shot Bethany, she looked me in the eyes and saw something evil there. She said it wasn't her son. According to her, I looked at her as though I was possessed by something. She felt a demon was looking at her through my eyes. She said that the next time she saw me, it was gone.

Being a twelve-year-old kid locked up with fourteen- to seventeen-year-olds, I had to grow up fast. I learned to keep to myself and stay quiet, blend into the background so I wouldn't be noticed. Surrounded by staff who could care less and a bunch of delinquent kids, I had to figure out most things on my own. I went through so much counseling, I couldn't stand it anymore; I quickly learned to say what the counselors wanted to hear and watched as they passed on to someone else.

Nothing was fixed inside me, and the inner battles remained. I had so much pain, grief, and hatred that I began hurting myself by hitting walls and making razor burns on my hands and arms. I knew that I deserved to hurt. When I punished myself, I felt better for a little while but not for long. Feeling better only made me feel worse.

When I was sixteen, with one year of my sentence left to serve, I was allowed to have a guitar, and I started teaching myself how to play. My plan, once I got out, was to become a biker, hang out in bars, and get into fights. That's all I wanted. Human life meant nothing to me, so why do anything else other than drink and fight? Yet something was happening. People I didn't know continually came to visit me and to talk to me about God. It happened so often I began to wonder if God was really real. They sure seemed convinced. They didn't judge me the way everyone else did. These visitors also looked genuinely happy, and I was very curious about what made them different. I started having a faint hope during their visits. But my hopes would fade quickly the moment I went back to my cell.

One day a woman I had never seen showed up to visit me. She gave me a Bible and sat and prayed with me. She visited a couple of times a month, and I liked her. I also liked to listen to the group of bikers—the Christian Motorcyclist Association—who came to the jail once a month for Bible studies. The first seeds of my interest in God were beginning to take root. My parents, of course, never stopped praying for me. Our church never stopped praying, both for me and for my family. Even in my confinement, God was there with me. God was there, even in my darkness.

After I was released from jail, I went back home to start my senior year of high school. It was a difficult transition, to say the least. I had to move back into the very house where I had killed my sister. Her room had been remodeled, so it was bigger and did not look as it did before I was sent to prison, but I still felt uneasy being there. I didn't feel that I belonged—neither in the house nor with my parents. I didn't know them as my mom and dad. I knew they had forgiven me, and they welcomed me home with open arms, but the last five years away from them had caused an emotional separation. The things I had learned about being a teenager, I learned from the older kids in the cells next to me. A friend in jail taught me how to shave. Things boys normally learn from their fathers, I did not learn from mine. I avoided talking at all about Bethany with my parents or anybody, for that matter. How could anyone look into the eyes of the people whose daughter's life you took? I couldn't.

But at school something was different. Before, I had felt totally alone. But now I felt accepted by some of the students. I even hooked up with a few of my old friends. I started drinking and smoking weed with them and then taking speed to stop myself from crashing. I would wake up some mornings with my heart pounding in my chest as if it were going to explode.

I would drive the seven miles in and out of town, from and back to our home, drunk and high, but I never once got in an accident, not even when snow and ice covered the roads and accidents claimed others' lives. I often had no recollection of even making the drive. God was looking out for me.

And how did I repay him? I ventured into some very ungodly things. I hated myself, and I learned to cut my arms with knives and burn myself with lighters. Even though I had served my time, I thought I still needed to be punished. I cut my left wrist deep enough that I severed the nerve and tendon, losing all feeling in two of my fingers.

My wake-up call came after I stole a pistol from a room in

the hotel where I worked. I faced a felony charge for posses-
sion of a weapon by a previous offender. The district attorney
wanted to throw me in prison for a long time. But by God's
grace my attorney got me three years' probation without any
jail time. That is when I knew—something had to change
right then, or I was done. I decided I needed a fresh start with
new friends, so I left town and moved in with a woman who
is now my wife. I still smoked weed and drank but quit using
speed. I met some bikers, who happened to be Christians, and
one night they invited me to church. I was married by that
time, but my wife did not want to go. I went. I was desperate.

As the pastor was saying a closing prayer, a rush of emo-
tion suddenly just hit me square on. All the feelings I had
held in for so long—all the people I had hurt, the lives I had
messed up—all of it began to surface. I was crying, and I
couldn't stop. I got up to leave, but my friend stopped me and
called the pastor over.

I told him everything. I told him about the hatred, the
stealing, the fighting, the drugs, and about killing my little
sister. I had nothing left to hide. I thought he might reject me
because of all the awful things I had done; he wouldn't have
been the first. But, instead, he asked me to pray. He asked me
to admit that I had done wrong, tell it all to God, ask him for
forgiveness, and accept that his Son, Jesus Christ, had died so
I no longer would have to face the consequences I deserved.
Those words changed my life forever. From that moment on
I was forgiven.

Forgiveness changes everything, but it is not a miracle
drug. Life was hard, and I had to face the consequences of
my choices, in my marriage, my heart, and my soul. Not a

single day goes by that I do not think about my sister. Even as far as God has brought me, there are still days that are difficult to get through. When I look at my past, I know that I am a murderer, a liar, a thief, and an adulterer. I've had idols before God, cursed his name, and degraded my parents. But my story does not end there. My story is not defined by my crimes or my sins. My story is defined by the rescue of God—the forgiveness, love, and grace he has poured into me.

If my tragic story shows anything, it is this: no matter how bad or messed up our lives may be, there is hope. Always, there is hope. It doesn't matter how many crimes we have committed or how many people we have hurt in the process. Jesus always offers hope. No matter how much hatred we have endured or pain we have inflicted, God always gives us hope. He loves us unconditionally, regardless of our messed-up lives.

Jesus died so that we don't have to. There is no better sacrifice than that. We just need to ask for forgiveness of our sins, believe in our hearts that Jesus died and that God raised him from the dead, and follow Jesus as our Lord and Savior. Do it, and your life will never be the same. Do it, and see for yourself what it means to live an adventure scripted by God himself.

Afterword

We chose "Redeemed" as the last story in *It's a God Thing* because we truly believe the most amazing miracle of all is that God saves people, just like Paul, every day, and that the three greatest words in all the world are *I love you*—which God so eloquently says to us through the gift of His Son.

> For God so loved the world that He gave His only begotten Son, that whoever believes in Him should not perish but have everlasting life. (John 3:16 NKJV)

For any reader who does not have a relationship with God through Jesus, we pray that these stories have persuaded you of His love and His power in the lives of His children and that you will come to know and love Him as we do.

And for you, our sisters and brothers who are experiencing difficult circumstances . . . in the book of Job there is a verse that speaks of courage that comes from hope (Job 11:18 NLT). It is our prayer that these stories infuse you with the hope that comes from a relationship with Jesus and the courage to live your life for His glory.

About the Writer

Craig Borlase is a writer living in the UK. He has co-authored twenty-one books, working with Tim Chaddick, Matt Redman, and many of the best-known worship songwriters. He has also written five solo books, including *The Naked Christian*; *William Seymour: A Biography*; and *2159 AD: A History of Christianity*.

Born in 1972, Craig grew up attending church, editing a Christian magazine, and eventually becoming a little cynical about things he really didn't understand.

"It was about the time when the organization I was involved with grew really big that I felt the need to write something that exposed what I saw as the problems with the church. It turned out that I was wrong: *The Naked Christian* was all about my own problems—my narrow view of faith, my weakness, my inconsistency, my arrogance."

After a two-year break to teach high school English, Craig

spent his early thirties working on his own books as well as writing for an international development agency. The experiences dramatically shaped his faith, as did the rites of birth and bereavement as his family grew at one end and shrank at the other.

"I feel as though I spent my teens trying to get a buzz out of faith (or drugs), my twenties waiting around for someone to give me permission to take faith seriously, and my thirties stripping away the nonsense and discovering the power of God's grace and love for myself.

"Being the only child of a single parent, the death of my mother was something I had long feared. Yet, like new growth after a bush fire, grief has given way to new life. These days I am excited about the journey that lies ahead and in awe of the way God weaves his great story into the lives of his children."

Today Craig writes collaboratively with a range of publishers and authors. His latest project tells the story of a young woman's record-breaking attempt to row across the Atlantic Ocean in the hope of raising awareness of the extent of human trafficking.

About the Creators

Don Jacobson has enjoyed working in the publishing industry for more than thirty years. After selling Multnomah Publishers to Random House in 2006, Don founded D. C. Jacobson & Associates (DCJA), an author management company, where he continues to work closely with authors—together dreaming about books that change the world by helping the church realize its true calling. Don's first collection of stories, *When God Makes Lemonade: True Stories That Amaze & Encourage*, was published by Thomas Nelson in 2013.

A graduate of Multnomah University in Portland, Don lives with Brenda, his wife of thirty-six years, in Portland, Oregon. They have four adult children.

K-LOVE creates compelling media that inspires and encourages listeners to have a more meaningful relationship with Christ. Our hope is that what you experience through

K-LOVE will deepen your relationship with Christ and help you understand His love for you and the amazing purpose that He has for your life.

> "For I know the plans I have for you," declares the LORD, "plans to prosper you and not to harm you, plans to give you hope and a future." (Jer. 29:11 NIV)

The radio network has 500 signals in 47 states, with an estimated weekly audience of 14 million. For more information visit www.klove.com.

WE WANT TO HEAR YOUR STORY . . .

Did reading these miracle stories help you remember a time that God acted—perhaps in your life? Maybe it's time to share that story—it just may be the thing someone needs to give him or her the courage to hang on and believe in God for a miracle.

SO WHAT IS YOUR GOD THING STORY?

It's always encouraging to hear stories of God at work in our lives, and we can't wait to hear yours! If you have never written anything, don't let that stop you—we have a writer who will help you tell your story.

If you would like to submit a story to be considered for our next volume of *It's a God Thing*, please visit our website at http://itsagodthing.com.

You can also follow us on Twitter (@IAGTMiracles) or like us on Facebook (http://facebook.com/itsagodthingmiracles).

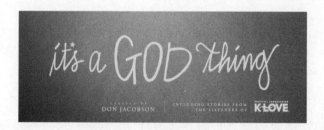

It's a God Thing stories are modern-day miracle stories—stories that simply can't be explained in any other way other than it was God's divine intervention.

K-LOVE: It IS a God Thing

God things are unexplainable. God things are also miraculous, wonderful, life affirming, and soul sustaining.

Clearly, what began humbly in 1982, as a single radio station in Santa Rosa, California, and has grown to a media empire of more than 500 stations from coast to coast that inspires more than 15 million listeners each week *is* a God thing. By providing positive music and inspirational stories, K-LOVE helps people draw closer to God, know God, and walk through every day of their lives *with* God.

Music is our tool, but the message of K-LOVE is far greater. Our mission is to effectively communicate the gospel to those who do not know or fully understand it while also helping those walking with Jesus Christ to grow stronger in their relationships with Him.

From music and inspirational stories to interviews with Christian artists and partnerships with Christian charities, K-LOVE is dedicated to serving Jesus Christ 24 hours a day, 7 days a week, 365 days a year, on-air and online. Behind the scenes K-LOVE's full-time ministry team processes more than one hundred phone calls a day from listeners seeking support and guidance. The pastors and staff at K-LOVE pray for more than a thousand prayer requests every day.

We are a ministry of believers with hearts for Jesus Christ and a love for serving others. We, like you, hear God through His Word and other believers whose personal testimonies showcase the powerful works He is doing in our lives. We hope this collection of stories will inspire you to look for God in your daily life, from your major triumphs, where His voice is loud and clear, to the small blessings, where His Holy Spirit quietly guides you to fulfill His purpose for your life.

K-LOVE creates compelling media designed to inspire and encourage people to develop meaningful relationships with Christ.

K-LOVE is listener supported and delivers positive, encouraging, contemporary Christian music through its five hundred signals across forty-seven states. For more information visit: www.klove.com.

POSITIVE, ENCOURAGING

K-LOVE

Connect with K-LOVE . . .

Website:	klove.com
Facebook:	Facebook.com/kloveradio
Twitter:	@kloveradio
Instagram:	@kloveradio
Google +:	+K-LOVE
Pinterest:	pinterest.com/kloveradio
YouTube:	youtube.com/kloveradio
Phone:	1.800.525.LOVE (5683)
Email:	klove@klove.com

*God is changing lives through Christian Radio –
thanks for sharing the vision!*

Our Values . . .

We Trust in God - Our faith, trust, and hope is in Christ. God's Word guides our decisions, refreshes us, and creates an unshakable faith. Our dependence on God is reflected in our commitment to prayer.

Create an Extraordinary Impact - We serve an extraordinary God who deserves our all. He allows us to create, produce, and share media with His life-changing message.

We are Passionate, Creative, and Have Fun - Innovative ideas and solutions, individual initiative, and having a good time make our work and lives more interesting.

Learn, Improve, and Grow - We challenge and stretch ourselves, each other, and the ministry to realize the full potential God has given us.

In His Strength - It's not about us.

Do you know someone who could use some encouragement? Perhaps that someone is you.

When God Makes Lemonade comes from the lives of everyday folk—a collection of stories about people like you who have discovered unexpected sweetness in the midst of sour circumstances.

Some of these real-life stories are laugh-out-loud funny, others are sobering, and more than a few will have you reaching for a tissue. But these true stories all have one thing in common: hope.

There is no question; life will sometimes give you *lemons*; out-of-your-control issues of health, employment, and relationships, circumstances that are truly sour—you wouldn't wish them on anyone.

But when those lemons become lemonade . . . it is as refreshing as an ice-cold drink on a hot summer day.

When in life "stuff happens," know that Lemonade Happens™ too! Be encouraged and inspired . . . *When God Makes Lemonade.*

If you have a Lemonade story to tell, please visit us at:

Website: www.godmakeslemonade.com
Facebook: www.facebook.com/godmakeslemonade
Twitter: @LemonadeHappens

THOMAS NELSON
Since 1798

thomasnelson.com

Available wherever books are sold